Is Your N

in the

Book of Life?

Introducing the Gospel
The only way to Heaven

Harold J Booth

IS YOUR NAME IN THE BOOK OF LIFE?

ISBN 978-1-908616-09-8

First Published 2012 by
Berforts Group Limited

Printed and bound in Great Britain by
www.berforts.com
Berforts Group, Stevenage

Introduction, Author's Notes and Abbreviations

Introduction

The primary aim of this book is to acquaint those who read it with the Book of Life, also called 'The Lamb's Book of Life,' mentioned in the Bible. A secondary aim is to show why it is essential that each reader's name should be written in it.

As no two readers will have the same Biblical knowledge and some might have very little, this book deals with all the matters that are necessary to explain why there is a Book of Life and the eternal and all-important consequences that will be the lot of those whose names are not written in it.

The Book of Life is in Heaven. Experience teaches that many do not realise that God can write, so this book acquaints its readers with the two occasions recorded in the Old Testament when God wrote, and the one occasion recorded in The Gospels when the Lord Jesus Christ wrote. These three occasions are discussed in the light of man's responsibility to God. As these occasions are also closely associated with the message of the Gospel, the Gospel is analysed and examined to see if the Gospel preached today is the same as that prophesied in the Old Testament and preached in New Testament days.

The comments in this book are based on the belief that the Bible is God's infallible word and it is through the Bible and only through the Bible that God speaks to us today. Because readers might assume that what they have seen or heard is true and based on the Bible, where religious doctrine, customs and practices, and popular notions and opinions are at variance with what the Bible teaches this book sets out those variances.

The comments in this book are also based on the belief that Jesus is the only way to Heaven. His own words, "I am the way and the truth and the life. No one comes to the Father except through me," tell us that if we believe in anyone else or anything else for Salvation, we shall not have our sins forgiven, enter Heaven, nor receive the blessings that God has for those who repent of their sins and believe in the Lord Jesus Christ.

Because this book contains comments on 'The Lamb's Book of Life,' the Gospel, Jesus and the way to Heaven, Salvation, forgiveness of sins and repentance, the reasons for Jesus' death and the blessings enjoyed by those who accept Him as Saviour and Lord are also mentioned.

Author's Notes

In this book capital letters have meaning and are used for references to God, the Lord Jesus Christ and the Holy Spirit. Gospel and Salvation are also capitalised because they are vital to an understanding of God's message for us.

Bible quotations are from the NIV Family of Bibles unless otherwise stated and we use the spelling and punctuation of the American English Bible from which we quote.

We refer to the Lord Jesus Christ as Jesus to remind us that Jesus means Saviour. He always was and always will be God the Son and the Son of God. God never asks us to understand eternal truths but He does expect us to believe them. Jesus was also the Jew's Messiah, the One that God promised in the Old Testament that He would send to them.

The first four books in the New Testament are The Gospels. They tell us about Jesus' birth, life, death, burial, resurrection and ascension and what Jesus did and taught. 'Gospel' means good news about the Salvation we can have if we repent and believe the Gospel. To save confusion, we refer to the four written Gospels as 'The Gospels.' The Gospel also refers to the message about Jesus and how, though sinners, we can have Salvation. We use the word 'Gospel' to refer to this message.

Parts of this book will be published separately hence there is some repetition. This is especially applicable to those parts dealing with Salvation and the reason for Jesus' death, burial and resurrection.

Abbreviations

ACTS: The Acts of the Apostles

CEV: Contemporary English Version

ERV: East-to Read Version

GB: GOD'S WORD

GNB: Good News Bible.

NIV: The NIV Family of Bibles

FOREWORD

By Dr Derek Stringer

National Director

Good News Broadcasting

Harold Booth believes that The Book of Life has become a forgotten truth and he is determined to make it a primary truth again. This punchy book sets out to help people understand this great truth and live in the good of it.

Harold always writes in a clear and direct style and never ducks a difficulty. This down to earth book makes a useful tool to live wisely and well. It is also of value to anyone who wants to share their faith but struggles to know how.

Don't read it if you don't want to be challenged as well as enlightened. I was both – and I appreciated it.

Dr Derek Stringer

National Director

Good News Broadcasting Association

Good News Broadcasting Association (GB)

Ranskill DN22 8NN United Kingdom

E-mail: info@gnba.net internet www.gnba.net

THE BOOK OF LIFE

The Bible teaches that 'The Book of Life' contains the names of those, and only those, who will be in Heaven.

Question: Did you know that:

- God can write?
- God has written to men?
- There is a Book in Heaven called, 'The Book of Life?'

As you read on you will discover what God has already written and what God is writing day by day.

Question: Do you know what God wants to write but He cannot do so without your consent? Answer: God wants to put your name in the Book of Life. The Book of Life contains the names of those who have accepted God's Salvation. Their names were added when they:

- Acknowledged to God that they were sinners.
- Repented of their sin.
- Turned their backs on their old way of life.
- Accepted Jesus as their Saviour and Lord.

God cannot write your name in the Book of Life unless and until you accept Jesus as your Saviour and Lord. As you read you will discover that God has chosen some fairly unusual ways to write to men. But one thing is certain. Those who ignore what God writes do so at their own peril. We usually commit important messages to writing and what God writes is of no less importance.

God's Law: The Ten Commandments

You will recall that God wrote His Law on two stone tablets and gave them to Moses. We read that 'The LORD said to Moses,' "Come up to me on the mountain. Stay here. I will give you the stone tablets. They contain the law and commands I have written to teach the people." Exodus 24:12. Moses came down from Mount Sinai with the two stone tablets and found that the Israelites were already disobeying what God had written on them. In anger Moses smashed the tablets. God replaced them. God had written, 'Do not put any other gods in place of me. Do not make statues of gods that look like anything in the sky or on the earth or in the waters. Do not bow down to them or worship them. I, the LORD your God, am a jealous God. I punish the children for the sin of their parents. I punish the grandchildren and great-grandchildren of those who hate me. But for all time to come I show love to all those who love me and keep my commandments. Do not misuse the name of the LORD your God. The LORD will find guilty anyone who misuses his name. Remember to keep the Sabbath day holy. Do all of your work in six days. But the seventh day is a Sabbath in honor of the LORD your God. Do not do any work on that day. The same command applies to your sons and daughters, your male and female servants, and your animals. It also applies to any outsiders who live in your cities. In six days I made the heavens and the earth. I made the oceans and everything in them. But I rested on the seventh day. So I blessed the Sabbath day and made it holy. Honor your father and mother. Then you will live a long time in the land the LORD your God is giving you. Do not commit murder. Do not commit adultery. Do not steal. Do not give false witness against your neighbor. Do not long for anything that belongs to your neighbor. Do not long for your neighbor's house, wife, male or female servant, ox or donkey.' Exodus 20:3-17.

To put the Ten Commandments into their Biblical context, we need to grasp what God said to Moses about His Law. "I will give you the stone tablets. They contain the law and commands I have written to teach the people," Exodus 24:12. What God said teaches us that the Law was obligatory and God wanted His Law taught. The Israelites could not pick and choose which of God's Laws they obeyed and which they disobeyed because:

- God would hold them to account for their disobedience.
- God regarded any disobedience as sin.

A Problem for the Disobedient

God has not changed His attitude to disobedience. He still regards all disobedience as sin or unrighteousness. He requires that His Law be taught even though teaching about disobedience is not popular with those who want to please themselves how they live. Many do not want to hear that:

- They will have to account to God for their sins.
- Unless forgiven, they will face God's judgment and the Lake of Fire which is frequently referred to as Hell and the name we shall use in this book.

Many think that the preaching of God's judgment for sin only began centuries ago when people lived very simple lives. Many think it is outdated and has been replaced by the view that Hell does not exist and whatever we believe, even if we believe nothing, we are all going to Heaven our own way.

Paul wrote Romans 6:23. It sums up what the Bible says about sin and judgment. First, we mention his background:

- As he was on his way to Damascus he was converted. It totally changed him and his religious outlook.
- Instead of carrying out his intention of arresting Jesus' followers who were preaching the Gospel in Damascus, he accepted Jesus as his personal Saviour and Lord.
- Almost overnight he became a very courageous Gospel preacher and years later, in a letter sent to Rome he wrote, 'For the wages of sin is death but the gift of God is eternal life in Christ Jesus our Lord.' Romans 6:23.

Paul contrasts 'the wages of sin' with 'the gift of God:'

- A wage is earned. A wage is not a gift.
- If we work for something, it cannot be a gift.
- A wage cannot be a gift.
- A gift cannot be a wage.

We are paid a wage for sinning. The wage is death. There is an alternative to being paid the wages of death for sinning. God wants to give us eternal life. But note that:

- We are not entitled to eternal life as of right.
- We cannot work for eternal life.
- We can only receive eternal life as a gift from God.

Question: Have you accepted God's gift of eternal life?

Note that Paul makes it quite clear that God's gift of eternal life is only available 'in Christ Jesus our Lord.' It is those vital words, 'in Christ Jesus our Lord,' that will:

- have a profound impact on your life now.
- determine your eternal destiny in Heaven or Hell.

It is those five words which now and for eternity divide mankind into two groups. But, before considering them, we consider why Paul chose to use the special title of:

Christ Jesus

There are many Names for Jesus in the Bible. Christ Jesus, is not mentioned before His resurrection and ascension. His Names of Jesus and Christ are written in two distinct ways:

- 'Jesus Christ' when His manhood is being emphasised.
- 'Christ Jesus' when His divinity is being emphasised.

Paul calls Jesus 'Christ Jesus our Lord,' not just 'Lord'. He emphasises that it is possible for us to possess Christ Jesus. If He is your Lord:

- You belong to Christ Jesus now and for eternity.
- Christ Jesus belongs to you now and for eternity.

If you never accept Christ Jesus as your Lord, you will be in His presence on Judgment Day but because He is not your Lord, you will face Him as your Judge. He will not welcome you into Heaven. He will send you to Hell.

The majority choose not to receive eternal life or the blessings that God wants to give those who put their trust in Jesus. God will not give eternal blessings to those who refuse to accept His Son Jesus as their Lord and Saviour.

Many only know about Jesus' birth, miracles and death. So it needs stressing that although Jesus died for our sins, death could not stop Him from becoming alive again. Why? Death claims us because we sin. Jesus was sinless and death had no power to stop Him becoming alive again.

Jesus preached that He came to seek and to save those who were lost, to be punished for our sin, to shed His blood and die so that those who put their trust in Him can:

- be redeemed so that they cease to be the slaves of sin.
- be totally and eternally forgiven by God.
- have the assurance of an eternal life in Heaven.

To confirm that there was nothing further that He needed to do to save us from God's judgment for sin, Jesus cried, "Finished" before He died. When Jesus became alive again, as He had already finished the work that His Father had given Him to do on earth, He returned to Heaven.

Two separate groups were referred to earlier.

The First Group

They have not repented and accepted Jesus as their Saviour and Lord. Christ Jesus is not their Lord. They have not received God's gift of eternal life. They remain unforgiven sinners. They will receive God's eternal punishment for their sin. Eternal death in Hell is the wage they have worked for.

The Second Group

They have received God's gift of eternal life as Christ Jesus is their Saviour and Lord. They heard the Gospel. They responded to its invitation to repent and accept Jesus as Saviour and Lord. As Jesus was punished and died for their sin, God can and has forgiven them. They will be in Heaven for eternity. They will never face God's judgment for sin, eternal death in Hell.

A Problem for Those Who Try to Obey the Law

Having considered the problem of those who disobey God, you might be surprised to learn that there can also be problems for those who seek to obey the Law. One serious problem concerns those who do their utmost to obey the Law believing that by doing so they will be on good terms with God and be in Heaven when they die. Before Paul trusted Jesus for God's Salvation, he did his utmost to obey the Law. He thought that by doing so he would please God and obtain eternal life. But after he put his trust in Jesus he realised how wrong his religious doctrine and practices and his attitude to God had been. So he made it clear in the verses quoted below that seeking to obey the Law cannot result in any one being 'right with God.' Paul wrote these words about the Law,

'Its purpose is to shut every mouth and make the whole world accountable to God. So it can't be said that anyone will be made right with God by obeying the law. Not at all! The law makes us more aware of our sin. But now God has shown us how to become right with him. The Law and the Prophets give witness to this. It has nothing to do with obeying the law. We are made right with God by putting our faith in Jesus Christ. That happens to all who believe...Everyone has sinned. No one measures up to God's glory. The free gift of God's grace makes all of us right with him. Christ Jesus paid the price to set us free. God gave him as a sacrifice to pay for sins. So he forgives the sins of those who have faith in his blood.' Romans 3: 19-25.

Despite the fact that Paul wrote these words some two thousand years ago, those who evangelise still need to emphasise why God wrote His Law and gave it to Moses. Sadly, there prevails a view that the Bible is 'out of date' and has not 'kept up with the times.' But the fact is that many with no Bible based beliefs are vulnerable to the most unbelievable man-made notions. The problem is widespread as so many hold the opinion that all beliefs are equally valid and all are entitled to their own beliefs or to have no beliefs. But what God writes and demands that it be taught can never be a matter of man's opinion. So no matter what you or I or mankind in general thinks:

- The Law was given to be obeyed and taught.
- Disobedience of the Law is sin.
- Only two choices exist. We either obey or we disobey.

The reason God wrote His Law is clearly stated, 'Its purpose is to shut every mouth and make the whole world accountable to God.' Romans 3:19.

'Shut Every Mouth'

'Make the Whole World Accountable to God'

'Shut Every Mouth:' God did not enter into any discussions with man as to which commandments He should or should not include before He wrote His Law. Man had no input in God's Law. If every mouth is shut, man's views about the Law are irrelevant. Men must accept the Law as it is.

‘Make the Whole World Accountable to God:’

- Sin is first and foremost disobedience to God.
- Sinners will account to God for their disobedience.
- God will punish unforgiven sin.

Does doing our best to obey the Law benefit us by making us right with God or providing us with forgiveness when we sin?

Paul answers this question emphatically. It is as though he knew that despite what the Bible teaches about God’s judgment for sin, there would be those who think that God should and will take good works into account when deciding the eternal future of those who do their best to obey His Law. So Paul states, ‘So it can't be said that anyone will be made right with God by obeying the law. Not at all! The law makes us more aware of our sin.’ Romans 3:20.

‘More Aware of Our Sin’

God wrote on two stone tablets and He said, “They contain the law and commands I have written to teach the people.”

Question 1: What did God want to teach the people?

Question 2: Why did God give Moses His Law?

Many might assume that God wanted to teach the people how they should behave towards Him and one another. But Paul’s teaching in Romans 3:19-25 makes it clear that the correct answer contains three truths. God wanted to:

- Shut every mouth.
- Make the whole world accountable to Him.
- Make us more aware of our sin.

When we considered the first two truths above we noted that:

- The Law is obligatory. It is not the basis for a discussion. It must be taught as God commanded. Men’s views or opinions of it are irrelevant. In fact, the fewer words spoken about disobeying the Law the better because everyone ought to keep their mouths’ shut.
- God will require us to account for our disobedience. Unlike man’s standards that vary from generation to

generation, God's standards and His Law are eternal.

'The Law Makes Us More Aware of Our Sin'

The first two truths in Romans 3:19-25 will not surprise many but the third truth cannot be well-known because many:

- who know that they fall short of God's righteous standard object to being classified as 'sinners.' They prefer to consider themselves as 'right with God' because they do their best to obey His Law.
- think that they are acceptable to God and will be in Heaven because they cannot do better than their best.

Sadly, although God wanted to teach us that as we cannot stop breaking His Law, we are sinners, many preach that doing our best is good enough for God. But God has set the standard. If we do not reach God's perfect standard we fail.

Consider a popular everyday test, the driving test. Those who fail the driving test are not classed as competent drivers by the Driving Standards Agency. It does not matter how good a driver we think we are, how good others tell us we are, or how hard we tried to drive correctly to pass the test. The driving test produces one of two results, 'pass' or 'fail.' There is no third for those who do their best. If our best effort is not up to the required standard, we fail. No one disputes this. But when God sets the standard in His Law, many choose to substitute their own standard. Think of the driving test again. Those who fail can be retested. A close friend fails the driving retests time after time. How long would it be before you said that they should stop wasting money on lessons and retests and accept the fact, the reality, that they will never be competent drivers?

The same reasoning applies to the Law. Our constant failure to obey should tell us that we do not and never will meet God's standard of perfection. Only Jesus did that.

The Law and Our Sin

We could consider the Ten Commandments individually but Jesus indicated that in essence there were two. He said the first one was the greatest and He blended the contents of the remaining nine into those famous words, 'Love your neighbour as yourself.' We read, '"Love the Lord your God with all your heart and with all your soul and with all your mind. This is the first and greatest commandment. And the second is like it. Love your neighbor as yourself."' Matthew 22:37-39. How many could claim that:

- God always has first place in their lives?
- They love God more than anyone or anything else?

Is it true that families, jobs and leisure take so much time in our lives that God is relegated to an hour or so on a Sunday? If you can say that you have always loved God with all your heart, soul and mind, and you have loved your neighbour as yourself, then you have lived as Jesus lived. Not only did He not sin, He could not sin. Both those who loved Him and those who hated Him could not find sin in Him. There are many religions in the world but their founders and leaders do not claim sinlessness.

- None of the great men of the Bible, such as Moses, Elijah, Isaiah, Peter, John and Paul claimed sinlessness.
- Readers of the Bible know that God has not hidden the sins of those we read about.
- Only Jesus could truthfully claim to have obeyed the Law.

Our Obedience to God

If we test our obedience to God by the two commandments mentioned by Jesus, we do not love God and our neighbours as we should. We continually disobey God. If we regularly and continually failed the driving test, we would know that our driving was not up to the required standard. How many times do we have to sin before we realise that we are sinners as:

- We regularly and so easily disobey the Law?
- We do not maintain God's standard?

So, as Paul wrote, 'the law makes us more aware of our sin.' It keeps on telling us that we are sinners.

Paul's Bad News

'So it can't be said that anyone will be made right with God by obeying the law.' Romans 3:20. That is the opposite of

Paul's belief before his conversion. And he was so sure in his unconverted days that his religion and his religious views were right that he executed Jesus' disciples who disagreed with him and preached the Gospel. But, there came a time in Paul's life when he realised two important truths:

- The Law was given to teach us that we were sinners.
- Faith in Jesus' sacrificial death makes us right with God.

What a difference his being made right with God made in Paul's life and in his preaching. Read again Romans 3:19-25; 6:23 above. They are the words of a converted law keeper. Let us suppose that after reading Paul's words, 'the law makes us more aware of our sin,' you realise that:

- You are an unforgiven sinner.
- Doing your best to live a good life will neither please God nor entitle you to a home in Heaven.

If after reading about sin and judgment you decide that:

- You do not want to remain an unforgiven sinner.
- You want to be right with God.
- You want Jesus to save you.

Paul states three truths that you need to believe:

- 'God has shown us how to become right with him.'
- 'It has nothing to do with obeying the law.'
- 'We are made right with God by putting our faith in Jesus…' So, if you want to be saved:
  - stop putting your faith in what you can do.
  - put your faith in what Jesus Christ has done for you.

Jesus Christ

He was both man and God. There is a reason why Paul uses Jesus' earthly Name first:

- God is immortal. He cannot die. So He became man so that He could die on behalf of sinners.
- Sinners deserve to be punished for their own sin so one sinner cannot die on behalf of other sinners and obtain

forgiveness for them. Jesus was sinless. He could take the punishment for our sins when He suffered and died.

- Jesus was sinless. Death had no claim on Him. He died voluntarily. Death could not stop Him coming back to life.

We sin and unless we accept God's free gift of eternal life, we will receive the wage that sin pays which is death. In total contrast, we mention again that because death had no claim upon Jesus, He came back to life. His miraculous resurrection proved that He was the holy Son of God.

A Word of Caution

Some think that Jesus died as a martyr. This and similar notions about Jesus' death that have no Biblical basis are mentioned in sermons but you will listen in vain for the truth about man's sin and God's eternal punishment to be included in many of them. The facts of Jesus' resurrection and ascension are, like His birth and death, the subject of man's disbelief. It seems that many have a desire to change the miraculous into an everyday event. Jesus is regularly demeaned. The majority do not believe that He always was and always will be God's Son who was crucified, came back to life and is now exalted in Heaven.

Question: Why should those who speak evil against the divine things that they do not understand, tremble? Answer: In the penultimate book of the Bible Jude tells us what these speakers do and their eternal future, '...those people speak evil things against what they don't understand.' 'God has reserved a place of very black darkness for them. He will keep them there forever.' Jude 10 & 13.

But it was not only Jude who issued a warning to those who speak evil about spiritual things. Jesus did not mince His words about those who wore long robes as part of their religious duties. He warned His hearers to be wary of them. Jesus' words do not seem to be well known as many assume that those who wear 'religious clothes' must be spiritual and in consequence they listen to and accept what they preach.

'All the people were listening. Jesus said to his disciples, "Watch out for the teachers of the law. They like to walk around in long robes. They love to be greeted in the market places. They love to have the most important seats in the synagogues. They also love to have the places of honor at dinners. They take over the houses of widows. They say long prayers to show off. God will punish those men very much.'" Luke 20:45-47.

Jude and Jesus were candid about the sins mentioned in the verses above and the dreadful eternal punishment that God has already reserved for those who commit these sins. It would be difficult to find more unambiguous words. We too must be equally as forthright and honest in warning those who listen to 'those men' that they are being misled.

We need to stress that it is the appreciation of what Jesus did for totally unworthy Hell-deserving sinners and their personal faith in His death, burial and resurrection that distinguishes those who believe in Jesus and have eternal life from those who do not. We consider again Romans 3 that states the vital importance of 'putting our faith in Jesus Christ.' 'We are made right with God by putting our faith in Jesus Christ. That happens to all who believe...Everyone has sinned. No one measures up to God's glory. The free gift of God's grace makes all of us right with him. Christ Jesus paid the price to set us free. God gave him as a sacrifice to pay for sins. So he forgives the sins of those who have faith in his blood.' Romans 3:22-25.

- 'That happens to *all* who believe…'
- *'Everyone* has sinned. No one measures up …
- The free gift of God's grace makes *all of us….*'

Look at the words we have italicised, 'all,' 'everyone,' and 'all of us.' If you ask when and where people are saved, you will receive a variety of answers. Many were saved in Sunday School days. Some attended Bible based youth groups and summer camps and were saved in their teens. Many in their 20s and upwards were saved when they heard the Gospel preached at Sunday services, evangelistic events and open air services in public parks and on the beach. Some were saved when they heard the Gospel in prison. Some were on death row. Some were saved when they heard the Gospel for the first time after years of seeking the truth but not finding it in religion. Missionary work, pamphlets and books, radio and TV have all played their part in spreading the Gospel worldwide. We relate these facts as experience teaches that what Paul wrote, two thousand years ago, is true today. There is and there has only ever been one Salvation. It still is available to all who repent and accept Jesus as Saviour and Lord:

- Their domicile, upbringing or creed has no relevance. The Gospel's invitation has no barrier for nationality or colour.
- Whether they have been sentenced to death for horrific crimes or are well-behaved juveniles, has no relevance.
- Age, sex, education and status are also immaterial.

As the italicised words above so clearly tell us, because everyone has sinned, everyone needs God's Salvation.

'Christ Jesus paid the price to set us free.'

Slaves lived pitiable existences. They were bought and sold. Slaves could be redeemed, that is, bought and set free. This is what Paul refers to when he states that 'Christ Jesus paid the price to set us free.'

- We were slaves in bondage to our sin.
- We could not be free from our bondage as we could not stop sinning.
- We would die as we had lived, slaves to our own sin.

Jesus did for us what we could not do for ourselves. He bled and died for our sin. He can release us from sin's bondage and set us free. He paid with His own blood the redemption price that bought our release from the slavery of sin.

Christ Jesus and God's Plan of Salvation

Paul's final comments about Christ Jesus in Romans 3:19-25 deserve our attention. In just a few words he sums up what some refer to as, 'God's Plan of Salvation.' It is a good name, though not a biblical one, as the Bible teaches that it was God's eternal plan that Jesus would die at Calvary. Contrary to what many preach and teach, Jesus was not taken by surprise when the Jewish people turned against Him and handed Him over to the Romans for crucifixion. This is obvious from Paul's words, 'God gave him as a sacrifice to pay for sins and he forgives the sins of those who have faith in his blood.' Romans 3:25.

When you read Romans 3:25, you realise that the religious beliefs and practices of so many cannot be supported by the Bible. This shows why you should read the Bible for yourself and not rely on what others say about it. Your eternal future is involved. There are two important expressions, 'to pay for sins' and 'he forgives the sins,' that we must consider:

'To pay for sins'

Many think that they can pay money to churches, charities and the like for forgiveness but Paul wrote, 'God gave him as a sacrifice to pay for sins.' So Paul tells us that the payment required for forgiveness has already been paid. Christ Jesus' sacrifice has already paid the price that God required:

- God does not want our money to pay for forgiveness.
- God wants us to have faith in the sacrifice that He gave.
- God's sacrifice was the death of Christ Jesus.

Many have been misled into believing that money and doing good will get them forgiveness. You need not remain misled and unforgiven. You now know from Paul how to obtain forgiveness so do not read on until you have been forgiven.

'He forgives the sins'

Only God can forgive sins. We have read about forgiveness and the sacrifice of Christ Jesus. Paul did not write about the:

- place where sins will be forgiven.
- church officials who need to be present.
- religious services during which forgiveness is available.
- procedures that have to be followed.
- contents of a written confession.

There is a simple reason for these omissions. They are totally unnecessary. Man's imagination and ingenuity has been at work over many centuries. Many have put their faith in man-made religions that have sprung up since New Testament days. Each one professes to be the true Church.

If you have put your faith in a religion, do what Paul says. Put your faith in the blood that Jesus shed for you. God will not forgive you until you do.

Those steeped in religion might find it difficult to accept the simplicity of Romans 3:25. So we repeat the verse and we:

- Consider those who are involved in God's forgiveness.
- Make the verse personal to yourself.

'God gave him as a sacrifice to pay for sins and he forgives the sins of those who have faith in his blood.' Romans 3:25.

The verse refers to, 'God,' 'him' and 'those.' Hence Paul wrote about God, Christ Jesus and us. If we personalise the verse it reads, God gave Christ Jesus as a sacrifice to pay for my sins and he will forgive my sins if I have faith in his blood. That is God's message for you today.

King Belshazzar

Sadly some think that they can ignore God and live as they please. We now consider one such man, King Belshazzar. His story, found in the Old Testament book of Daniel, is well worth reading. Keep in mind that God knows:

- The sins we commit.
- Those who are arrogant about their sin.
- Those who ignore His warnings.

He was Nebuchadnezzar's son. Nebuchadnezzar's army had ransacked Jerusalem capturing a vast number of Jews. Nebuchadnezzar learned from the Jews about the living and true God. God intervened in his life to prove to him that it is God and not man who 'rules over all of the kingdoms of men.' Belshazzar must have known about God's two interventions in his father's life:

- God's first intervention involved a furnace that could not burn three young Jews, Shadrach, Meshach and Abednego. Nebuchadnezzar personally ordered their deaths because they would not bow down to his idol.
- God also intervened to strip Nebuchadnezzar of his throne and he lived in the fields like an animal.

The Furnace: Shadrach, Meshach and Abednego

Extracts from Daniel 3: ‘At that time some people who studied the heavens came forward. They spoke against the Jews. They said, “King Nebuchadnezzar, may you live forever! You commanded everyone to fall down and worship the gold statue. You told them to do it when they heard the horns, flutes, zithers, lyres, harps, pipes and other musical instruments. If they didn't, they would be thrown into a blazing furnace. But you have appointed some Jews to help Daniel govern Babylon and the towns around it. Their names are Shadrach, Meshach and Abednego. They don't pay any attention to you, King Nebuchadnezzar. They don't serve your gods. And they refuse to worship the gold statue you have set up.” Nebuchadnezzar burned with anger. He sent for Shadrach, Meshach and Abednego. So they were brought to him. The king said to them, “Shadrach, Meshach and Abednego, is what I heard about you true? Don't you serve my gods? Don't you worship the gold statue I set up? You will hear the horns, flutes, zithers, lyres, harps, pipes and other musical instruments. When you do, fall down and worship the statue I made. If you will, that's very good. But if you won't, you will be thrown at once into a blazing furnace. Then what god will be able to save you from my powerful hand?” Shadrach, Meshach and Abednego replied to the king. They said, “King Nebuchadnezzar, we don't need to talk about this anymore. We might be thrown into the blazing furnace. But the God we serve is able to bring us out of it alive. He will save us from your powerful hand. “But we want you to know this. Even if we knew that our God wouldn't save us, we still wouldn't serve your gods. We wouldn't worship the gold statue you set up.” Then Nebuchadnezzar's anger burned against Shadrach, Meshach and Abednego. The look on his face changed. And he ordered that the furnace be heated seven times hotter than usual. He also gave some of the strongest soldiers in his army a command. He ordered them to tie up Shadrach, Meshach and Abednego. Then he told his men to throw them into the blazing furnace. So they were tied up. Then they were thrown into the furnace. They were wearing their robes, pants, turbans and other clothes. The king's command was carried out quickly. The furnace was so hot that its flames killed the soldiers who threw

Shadrach, Meshach and Abednego into it. So the three men were firmly tied up. And they fell into the blazing furnace. Then King Nebuchadnezzar leaped to his feet. He was so amazed he asked his advisers, “Didn't we tie three men up? Didn't we throw three men into the fire?” “Yes, we did," they replied. The king said, “Look! I see four men walking around in the fire. They aren't tied up. And the fire hasn't even harmed them. The fourth man looks like a son of the gods.” Then the king approached the opening of the blazing furnace. He shouted, “Shadrach, Meshach and Abednego, come out! You who serve the Most High God, come here!” So they came out of the fire. The royal rulers, high officials, governors and advisers crowded around them. They saw that the fire hadn't harmed their bodies. Not one hair on their heads was burned. Their robes weren't burned either. And they didn’t even smell like smoke. Then Nebuchadnezzar said, “May the God of Shadrach, Meshach and Abednego be praised! He has sent his angel and saved his servants. They trusted in him. They refused to obey my command. They were willing to give up their lives. They would rather die than serve or worship any god except their own God. “No other god can save people that way. So I'm giving an order. No one from any nation or language can say anything against the God of Shadrach, Meshach and Abednego. If they do, they'll be cut to pieces. And their houses will be turned into piles of trash.” Then the king honored Shadrach, Meshach and Abednego. He gave them higher positions in the city of Babylon and the towns around it.’

Nebuchadnezzar came up against God’s Will. It had negatived his will. He saw a fourth person in the furnace. So he said good things about God. But Nebuchadnezzar did not repent and change his ways. Experience teaches that many:

- Know about God, are reverent and do not blaspheme.
- Work for the church believing that they serve God.
- Can recite the Creed and various prayers that refer to God’s majestic power, holiness and goodness.
- Know all about Christmas and Easter and enthusiastically sing carols and hymns that celebrate these events.

But many who live honourably and admit in church services

that they have sinned have never been so sorry for their sin that they have repented and now live to please God. And many live as if Jesus had not been punished for their sins, and shed His blood and died on their behalf. The problem is:

- Many do what they think God requires them to do rather than doing what God actually requires them to do.
- Many obey either their own or their church's religious rules and they think that God should be satisfied with that.

God's Judgment upon Nebuchadnezzar

We know what Nebuchadnezzar said when he complimented God. But despite his personal experience of God's almighty power he remained proud. As we shall read later, God stripped him of his throne.

Belshazzar's Knowledge of God's Judgment for Sin

Belshazzar's knew that God judges sin but he was proud like his father. Both kings had benefited from employing Jews such as Daniel, Shadrach, Meshach and Abednego who, despite their deportation, remained faithful to God. Their godly lives were a constant reminder that God exists.

BELSHAZZAR'S FEAST

Extracts from Daniel 5: 'King Belshazzar gave a great banquet for a thousand of his nobles and drank wine with them…he gave orders to bring in the gold and silver goblets that Nebuchadnezzar his father had taken from the temple in Jerusalem, so that the king and his nobles, his wives and his concubines might drink from them…As they drank the wine, they praised the gods of gold and silver, of bronze, iron, wood and stone. Suddenly the fingers of a human hand appeared and wrote on the plaster of the wall, near the lampstand in the royal palace. The king watched the hand as it wrote. His face turned pale and he was so frightened that his legs became weak and his knees were knocking. The king summoned the enchanters, astrologers and diviners…but they could not read the writing or tell the king what it meant. So King Belshazzar became even more terrified and his face grew more pale. His nobles were baffled. The queen, hearing the voices of the king and his nobles, came into the banquet hall. "May the king live forever!" she said. “Don't be alarmed! Don't look so pale…Call for Daniel, and he will tell you what the writing means.” So Daniel was brought before the king…Daniel answered the king…“Your Majesty, the Most High God gave your father Nebuchadnezzar sovereignty and greatness and glory and splendor. Because of the high position he gave him, all the nations and peoples of every language dreaded and feared him…But when his heart became arrogant and hardened with pride, he was deposed from his royal throne and stripped of his glory. He was driven away from people and given the mind of an animal; he lived with the wild donkeys and ate grass like the ox; and his body was drenched with the dew of heaven, until he acknowledged that the Most High God is sovereign over all kingdoms on earth and sets over them anyone he wishes. But you, Belshazzar, his son, have not humbled yourself, though you knew all this. Instead, you have set yourself up against the Lord of heaven. You had the goblets from his temple brought to you, and you and your nobles, your wives and your concubines drank wine from them. You praised the gods of silver and gold, of bronze, iron, wood and stone, which cannot see or hear or understand. But you did not honor the God who holds in his hand your life and all your ways. Therefore he sent the hand that wrote the inscription. Here is what these words mean: MENE: God has numbered the days of your reign and brought it to an end. TEKEL: You have been weighed on the scales and found wanting. PERES: Your kingdom is divided and given to the Medes and Persians.” That very night Belshazzar…was slain…’

Daniel gives us a wonderful description of a terrified man. Why did God write to Belshazzar? What was his sin? Foolishly, he chose to ignore God’s warnings and decided to challenge God. Two matters in this story need our attention. One illustrates the problem that so many religious people have and the other the problem that we all have and why we all need God's Salvation.

King Belshazzar’s First Problem: He was proud

Romans 6:23 states that, ‘the wages of sin is death, but the gift of God is eternal life in Christ Jesus our Lord.’ Before writing these words, Paul asked this question, 'What benefit did you reap at that time from the things you are now ashamed of? Those things result in death!' Romans 6:21.

Who was Paul writing to?

In Romans 6:21 we read the pronoun, 'you.' When you read the Bible, read the pronoun 'you' with care. Some think that it applies to them. But the word 'you' could only apply to those to whom Paul was writing. If those he wrote to and you have everything in common, then what he wrote would also apply to you. Two examples will clarify this:

- Paul opens his letter to the Romans, 'To all in Rome who are loved by God and called to be his holy people: Grace and peace to you from God our Father and from the Lord Jesus Christ.' Romans 1:7. So when you read Romans, it is clear that the pronoun, 'you' does not refer to everyone who reads the letter. It only refers to the believers in Rome at that time.
- We quote Jesus' famous words from John 14:1-2. (AV) 'Let not your heart be troubled: ye believe in God, believe also in me. In my Father's house are many mansions: if it were not so, I would have told you. I go to prepare a place for you.' Jesus spoke only to His disciples. He referred to them as, 'you.' His words are often used to provide solace to grieving families but it cannot be right to pretend that Jesus was speaking to all and sundry when His words only apply to those who have believed in Him.

The Truth in Romans 6:21.

'What benefit did you reap at that time from the things you are now ashamed of? Those things result in death!'

Question: Who are the 'you?' Answer: Believers in Rome.

But it is not only the pronouns that are used in the Bible that require careful consideration. Also important are:

- The tenses.
- The time or the period of time that the verse refers to.

Paul refers to two periods of time in Romans 6:21. One is, 'at that time' and the other is, 'now.'

- 'At that time.' The period before each believer was saved.
- 'Now.' The period after each believer was saved.

We need to consider the periods of time in Romans 6:21, before we comment on the problem of pride.

Our Present and Past

Each one of us has a present and a past but for some, like Paul and the believers in Rome to whom he was writing:

- A change in their life and their lifestyle had occurred.
- They knew when and why this change had occurred.

The lifestyle change that is part of and essential to repentance is found throughout the Bible. True repentance is visible. Jesus said the well-known words, "by their fruits you shall know them." If we want to know if a tree is good or bad we taste its fruit. Our behaviour identifies what we are inside.

A good example is Paul's conversion. After his conversion at Damascus he returned to Jerusalem. He had been a cruel persecutor of the Jerusalem believers and they had every reason to be wary of him. They wondered if he really had been converted. But when Barnabas told them what Paul had done since his conversion and how that he had risked his life in his desire to preach the Gospel, they were reassured. When the Jerusalem believers looked at Paul they could not see that:

- He had repented.
- He had turned his back on his old way of life.

If you repent and believe in Jesus you will not change physically. The change that must occur will be on the inside:

- The Holy Spirit will indwell you and teach you spiritual truths and how to live a holy life that pleases God.
- You will realise the difference between things that please God and things that please men.
- You will see sin, especially your own sin, as God sees it.

The spiritual transaction that occurs when a person repents and accepts Jesus as Saviour and Lord cannot be seen by humans but what they should and must see is the external evidence of this spiritual transaction and that means a changed lifestyle. If that external evidence does not exist, it is unlikely that there has been a spiritual transaction. Some equate repentance with a simple resolve to improve or do better. 'New Year Resolutions' and the desire to 'turn over a new leaf' have nothing to do with repentance. Sadly many do not associate Salvation with a new lifestyle. After their alleged conversion they live as they have always done. But in Romans 6:21 Paul emphasises two truths.

- The first truth: When you looked at the lives of the believers you saw a change from how they behaved before they were saved and how they now behaved.
- The second truth: The believers were ashamed of their behaviour before they were saved.

Question: Has your lifestyle changed because you realised:

- God hates your sin.
- God gave Jesus as a sacrifice to pay for your sins?
- God only forgives those who have faith in Jesus' death?

Question: Was your lifestyle change based upon your decision that as Jesus was sacrificed for your sin you would:

- Confess to God that you were a sinner.
- Repent and turn your back on your sin.
- Accept Jesus as your Saviour and Lord.

Question: If there has not been a change in your lifestyle, could it be that you are not converted?

Question: Are you ashamed of the life you lived before you were saved? The believers in Rome were and it evidenced their Salvation. Those who are proud of their past lives need to ask themselves if they have been saved.

Sermons can be based on Bible verses that offend no one, with the result that some of Jesus' words recorded in The Gospels are little-known. We need to consider the background to Jesus' words in Luke 13. Luke writes that Jesus was walking to Jerusalem and He preached in the towns and the villages along the way. It seems that very few responded to His preaching. You can read in Luke 13:23-28 Jesus' answer to a perceptive question, "Lord, are only a few people going to be saved?" Jesus said, "'Try very hard to enter through the narrow door. I tell you, many will try to enter and will not be able to. The owner of the house will get up and close the door. Then you will stand outside knocking and begging. You will say, 'Sir, open the door for us.' "But he will answer, 'I don't know you. And I don't know where you come from. "Then you will say, 'We ate and drank with you. You taught in our streets.' "But he will reply, 'I don't know you. And I don't know where you come from. Get away from me, all you who do evil!' "You will sob and grind your teeth when you see those who are in God's kingdom. You will see Abraham, Isaac and Jacob and all the prophets there. But you yourselves will be thrown out."'

Jesus said, "Many will try to enter and will not be able to." Never think that the majority will be saved. Jesus said they will not. Consider the words of those refused admittance who thought that they should be allowed in and the replies they received. Their words were, "We ate and drank with you. You taught in our streets." Twice the owner replied, "I don't know you." You will now realise why this story is little known. We have no wish to offend but we cannot ignore the fact that many are misled into thinking that their place in Heaven is 'guaranteed.' Those listening to non-Bible based sermons are being deceived. Jesus had both friends and enemies. Some people listened to Him. Others opposed His preaching and planned His death.

Question: Did Jesus say, "I don't know you," to the people who ate with Him and heard Him preach or to His enemies?

Answer: Jesus' words were spoken to those who listened to Him. They said in their reply, "We ate and drank with you. You taught in our streets." Many would assume that the words, "I don't know you," would only be said to Jesus' enemies and not to churchgoers and the like? So we ask, will Jesus say those words to you? Could it be that like so many you have always assumed that your religion, religious observances and good works will guarantee you a place in Heaven? If you are proud of your past good deeds, we can tell you with Biblical authority that you are not saved.

The Pride of Religion and Good Works

Experience teaches that obedience to a religion and religious observances or a willingness to do good works can so easily produce pride. Many are proud of:

- ❖ Their religion and their own religious attainments.
- ❖ Their support to religious organisations and charities.
- ❖ Their good life and neighbourliness.
- ❖ Their efforts to keep the Commandments.

Our pride can act like a smokescreen to cover our sin. God sees through it. He sees what we really are, proud sinners. God wants to see humble repentant sinners that He can forgive. He wants to give them the spiritual blessings He has for all who accept Jesus as their personal Saviour and Lord.

Repentant sinners are not proud of their past life. How could they be proud of their past sinful behaviour when Jesus suffered and died for it on the cross?

- ❖ How could Jesus be the Saviour and Lord of anyone who still lived the same proud life that they had always lived?
- ❖ How could anyone claim to be saved and indwelt by the Holy Spirit and not live a new spiritual life?

If you accept Jesus as your Saviour and Lord, the Holy Spirit will immediately indwell you and teach you how to live to please a holy sin-hating God. The Holy Spirit, as His Name so clearly indicates, enables believers to achieve practical divine holiness. This must not be confused with the sin of 'self-righteousness.'

Belshazzar's Second Problem

We have considered Belshazzar's first problem, the sin of pride. It is a problem that stops many from being saved because they think that their lives are good enough for God. Some even say that they will get to Heaven their own way.

Belshazzar's second problem is commonplace. He might have been one of the most powerful men on Earth but to God he was an unsaved sinner. He was not ignorant of God's power and he was well aware of God's dealings with his father, Nebuchadnezzar. But neither father nor son repented.

Similarly many today know quite a lot of information about God and His dealings with mankind. Some do their best to follow their own or their churches' rules and they believe that God will be satisfied with their honest efforts to live a good life. But is God satisfied with our best efforts?

God's Judgment upon Belshazzar

Belshazzar knew of God's judgment upon Nebuchadnezzar. Daniel's words, sum up Belshazzar's attitude to God. "But you knew all of that...After all, you are Nebuchadnezzar's son. In spite of that, you are still proud. You have taken your stand against the Lord of heaven." Daniel 5:22-23.

Despite Belshazzar's knowledge of God's judgment, he was proud like his father. Both kings had benefited from employing Jews who remained faithful to God. Their lives were a constant reminder that God exists. Consider Belshazzar's wife's advice. She knew that God's prophet, Daniel could interpret the writing. Experience teaches that while many have seen God at work in the lives of others, they prefer to remain observers.

God's Message to Belshazzar: TEKEL.

Daniel told Belshazzar that 'TEKEL' meant, '"You have been weighed on the scales and found wanting."' Before we comment on 'Tekel,' we ask a question.

Question: Do rules state who will be in Heaven and how we get there? We hear at least four different answers:

Answer 1: There are no rules as everyone will be in Heaven.

Answer 2: We can make up and keep our own rules.

Answer 3: Our Church has laid down what the rules are.

Answer 4: God's rules apply.

Answer 4 is unchallengeable. Why are Answers 1-3 wrong?

Answer 1 is wrong. Even a cursory reading of The Gospels will prove that Jesus spoke more about Hell than He did about Heaven. Many are not aware of this. To believe that everyone will be in Heaven contradicts what Jesus taught.

Answer 2 is wrong. Many must think it is right as experience teaches that many have made up their own rules. They:

- apply logic and philosophy to the issue of good and evil.
- resolve that they will try to do good and avoid doing evil.
- conclude that God will be satisfied with their best efforts.

The problem with popular notions is that it cannot be other than foolish to ignore the fact that we all sin against a holy God. Many might think of sin only as 'naughtiness,' but God has never downgraded sin. God always has and always will hate our sin. Hence, in the Bible God refers to:

- wrongdoing as, 'evil.'
- those who do wrong as, 'the wicked.'

King David the psalmist had no illusions about God's holiness and hatred of sin. Sin makes God angry and although He might not instantly punish it, we must not let that fool us into thinking that He ignores or overlooks it. As we read Psalm 7:11-13 David's words might initially seem out-of-date but no one will fail to grasp the fact that God's daily anger will one day result in His judgment against those who do not repent. David wrote: 'God judges fairly. He shows his anger every day. If evil people don't change their ways, God will sharpen his sword. He will get his bow ready to use. He has prepared his deadly weapons…'

If 'doing good and avoiding evil' had been the way to Heaven, it would not have been necessary for Jesus to die. Hence from Genesis to Revelation the Bible teaches that:

- Sin must either be forgiven or punished.
- Forgiveness is only available through shed blood.

We quote from the Old Testament. Isaiah tells us that Jesus, God's Servant, would one day suffer for sin. The New Testament verses, one from John, the other from Peter, tell us why Jesus came and why He was crucified:

ISAIAH: 'the servant was pierced because we had sinned. He was crushed because we had done what was evil. He was punished to make us whole again. His wounds have healed us. All of us are like sheep. We have wandered away from God. All of us have turned to our own way. And the Lord has placed on his servant the sins of all of us.' Isaiah 53:5-6.

JOHN: 'The Father has sent his Son to be the Savior of the world.' 1 John 4:14.

PETER: 'Christ also suffered once for sins, the righteous for the unrighteous, to bring you to God.' 1 Peter 3:18.

Answer 3 is wrong. How many assume that this answer must be correct as their church ought to know the answer? How many believe what their church teaches without giving the matter a second thought. It is not our wish to offend, but we cannot ignore facts. No one has a choice as to their initial involvement with any particular church. Their parents choose the church where they are christened. Thereafter they usually hear only the teaching of that church. The various churches have their own beliefs about Heaven. They cannot all be right. It seems very precarious for anyone to trust their church's teaching unless it teaches God's rules.

Answer 4 cannot be other than correct because God's rules as to who will be in Heaven and how we get there must apply. The following verses were once well known as many committed them to memory when young. They are Jesus' words and they tell us God's way to Heaven:

- '"For God so loved the world that he gave his one and only Son, that whoever believes in him shall not perish but have eternal life."' John 3:16.
- '"I am the way and the truth and the life. No one comes to the Father except through me."' John 14:6.

Question 1: Who decides if we will be in Heaven?

Question 2: Is it a final decision?

Question 3: Is the decision made before or after we die?

These questions will be answered as we look at 'TEKEL,' meaning, 'You have been weighed on the scales and found wanting.' Daniel told Belshazzar that God knew his sins and he was going to be punished by death for two specific sins:

Sin 1: He had 'set himself up against the Lord of Heaven.'

Sin 2: He had not 'humbled himself.'

Belshazzar sins have to be viewed in the light of Daniel's words to him about God's judgment of his father. Daniel said to him, "you knew all this." We know that Belshazzar was proud but he was also foolish. He made a decision to publicly challenge God. He used the sacred Jewish Temple goblets to worship idols and he encouraged others to do the same. Foolhardy might be more apt to describe his self-important irreverent attitude to God. However we describe him, he was first and foremost proud. His pride resulted in his downfall.

God's Dealings with Belshazzar and His Sin of Pride

We know from the Bible that God hates all sin but it is the sin of pride that is singled out for condemnation throughout the Bible. We humans have a tendency to categorise sin so that we think of murder as more serious than assault and burglary more serious than pickpocketing. Few would include pride on a list of serious sins. But as pride stops many admitting that they are sinners and seeking God's forgiveness, it might be that pride is the sin that in reality condemns many to an eternal Hell. As you read on, you will see that God's dealings with Belshazzar are enlightening and well worth studying.

The expression, 'weighed on the scales' proves that God is not capricious. In Psalm 7 that we read earlier, David wrote, 'God judges fairly.' His decisions are not made by impulse or whim. He knew all about Belshazzar. He knows all about us.

- His subjects saw a proud and powerful man, a man who liked to impress friend and enemy alike and a man who would spare no expense to draw attention to himself.
- God saw one of His sinful creatures publicly challenging His authority, publicly declaring that he preferred to worship idols and encouraging others to do the same.
- God reacted to Belshazzar's sins. Despite his power and wealth, God publicly announced to him that there was something that was lacking in his life. We are not told what it was as Daniel only told him his two sins.

Was Belshazzar's challenge of God unique? Maybe, but we cannot imagine anyone denying that pride is not widespread. We have spent time considering the writing on the wall because experience teaches that those words, 'you have not humbled yourself,' apply to so many that have not accepted God's forgiveness. Those who are saved look back on their past and are ashamed. Those who are not saved are proud of their past. So we repeat that pride is a sin that keeps so many from seeking forgiveness. It is a characteristic that God hates and Belshazzar's story teaches that God sees it.

Assumptions

We can assume that Belshazzar wanted to prove that he was superior to God in the presence of his Babylonian guests but did Belshazzar assume that God would ignore his challenge or that he was superior to God? Did he assume that the Temple goblets had no significance but if they did his idols were superior to God and they would protect him?

Making run-of-the-mill assumptions has to be part of our daily lives. We would do very little if we had to have proof that the end result of what we wanted to do would be successful before we started to do anything. Experience teaches that many make assumptions about God and divine matters that are contrary to what the Bible teaches. Making assumptions about spiritual matters is foolish. The Bible states all we need to know and can be so easily read. It states that human assumptions about divine matters will always be incorrect. Jesus taught that only those who are saved and possess the Holy Spirit are able to understand divine truth. So, as we read about Belshazzar's attitude to God, we will consider some of the assumptions that are made today and which Belshazzar's story shows us are incorrect.

False Assumption 1: God is Inactive Today.

False Assumption 2: God Will Judge Sin in the Future.

Belshazzar's story and the Bible show that God is anything but inactive or complacent about the sins we commit.

False Assumption 3: God is Only a God of Love

No doubt the vast majority want this assumption to be true but Belshazzar's punishment shows that it is false. It is true that God loves sinners but He hates sin. He will punish unrepentant sinners who ignore His forgiveness. The truth that God hates sin appears throughout the Bible. Take

Belshazzar's sin of pride. In the New Testament letters of both James and Peter, we read identical words about those who are proud. Both men refer to a truth that is found in the Old Testament book of Proverbs. Proverbs 3:34 is the last of three consecutive verses that tell us God's attitude to sin:

- 'For the LORD detests the perverse but takes the upright into his confidence.' Proverbs 3:32.
- 'The LORD's curse is on the house of the wicked, but he blesses the home of the righteous.' Proverbs 3:33.
- 'He mocks proud mockers but shows favor to the humble and oppressed.' Proverbs 3:34.

Consider the expressions in these three verses:

- Proverbs 3:32. 'the Lord detests…'
- Proverbs 3:33. 'the Lord's curse…'
- Proverbs 3:34. 'He mocks proud mockers…'

These words show that God is presently active against sin and sinners. It is God's present activity against the proud that James and Peter seek to emphasise. They write the same words. James 4:6 & 1 Peter 5:5 state, 'God opposes the proud but shows favor to the humble.'

Is it your pride that stops you admitting that you are a sinner who needs Jesus to save you from your sin? You will never be saved unless you admit that you are a sinner. It is the first step on the way to Heaven. This takes us back to the three questions we asked about the way to Heaven.

- Question 1: Who decides if we will be in Heaven?
- Question 2: Is it a final decision?
- Question 3: Is the decision made before or after we die?

Answers 1 & 2: We decide and it is final. God will not force us to repent and accept Jesus as our Saviour and Lord.

Answer 3: The notion that we will not know whether our future is in Heaven or in Hell until we have died is wrong. It is like the similar notion that God has some scales and after we die, He weighs our good and bad deeds. Maybe this idea has come from the reference to scales in Belshazzar's story. But,

Belshazzar was very much alive when Daniel said to him, “You have been weighed on the scales and found wanting.”

The Bible teaches that those who reject Jesus have already been judged and condemned. They are clearly very much alive as they have until they die the opportunity of being saved from this condemnation. Three verses, John 3:16-18, clarify this. ‘For God so loved the world that he gave his one and only Son, that whoever believes in him shall not perish but have eternal life. For God did not send his Son into the world to condemn the world, but to save the world through him. Whoever believes in him is not condemned, but whoever does not believe stands condemned already because they have not believed in the name of God's one and only Son.’ John 3:16-18.

Some assume that death ends our existence but Jesus said: “I am the resurrection and the life. Anyone who believes in me will live, even if he dies.” John 11:25. In two of his letters Paul wrote about believers who have died. Note how Paul refers to them and the words we have italicised:

- ‘who have fallen asleep *in Christ...’* 1Corinthians 15:18.
- ‘the dead *in Christ…’* 1Thessalonians 4:16.

We die in Christ or without Christ. No third option exists.

Before we move on to read the story of Jesus and the adulterous woman in John 8, we sum up what we have read in the Bible about God and our sin:

- Everyone is underweight. We are not good enough for God. Without exception we all sin. The degree to which we sin might vary, but sin is inherent in us. No one taught us to sin. Inherent sin is soon evident. From an early age we want our own way. We sin because we are sinners.
- But the good news of the Gospel is that Jesus was willing to be punished and die for our sins. Jesus was without sin. He bled and died so that we or anyone who is prepared to accept Him as Saviour and Lord can be cleansed of sin and forgiven. Only Jesus’ blood can wash away our sin and not only make us clean, but clean enough to enter Heaven.
- We cannot enter Heaven with our sin. Jesus did not come

into the world to condemn us. Our sin does that. Jesus came that we might be saved. The time to ensure that you do not suffer God's punishment is now. Salvation is available now. In 2 Corinthians 6:2 Paul quotes Isaiah 49:8 to stress that now is the time for action. Bible translators have sought to express this urgency. Three different translations tell you that God wants to hear from you now:

- CEV: 'This is the day for you to be saved.'
- ERV: 'The "day of salvation" is now.'
- GNB: 'I tell you that the "right time" is now. The "day of salvation" is now.'

You can refuse God's Salvation. You can choose to ignore God's 'handwriting on the wall' for you. You have no such choice as to God's judgment for your sin.

Jesus and the Adulterous Woman: John 8

Jesus was asked a trick question by the religious elite who tried to discredit Him. They thought that He would not be able to answer their question. They considered themselves wise but they were not wise enough to realise who Jesus was.

John 8:2-11.'All the people gathered around him there. He sat down to teach them. The teachers of the law and the Pharisees brought in a woman. She had been caught in adultery. They made her stand in front of the group. They said to Jesus, "Teacher, this woman was caught having sex with a man who was not her husband. In the Law, Moses commanded us to kill such women by throwing stones at them. Now what do you say?" They were trying to trap Jesus with that question. They wanted to have a reason to bring charges against him. But Jesus bent down and started to write on the ground with his finger. They kept asking him questions. So he stood up and said to them, "Has any one of you not sinned? Then you be the first to throw a stone at her." He bent down again and wrote on the ground. Those who heard what he had said began to go away. They left one at a time, the older ones first. Soon only Jesus was left. The woman was still standing there. Jesus stood up and asked her, "Woman, where are they? Hasn't anyone found you guilty?" "No one, sir," she said. "Then I don't find you guilty either," Jesus said. "Go now and leave your life of sin."'

We began this book by considering God's Law. God wrote His Law twice on stone tablets. Moses smashed the first stone tablets because the Israelites were actively disobeying the Law when he came down from Mount Sinai. We read that Jesus twice wrote on the ground with His finger. Exodus 31:18 leaves us in no doubt how God wrote His Law. 'The Lord finished speaking to Moses on Mount Sinai. Then he gave him the two tablets of the covenant. They were made out of stone. The words on them were written by the finger of God.' We do not know what Jesus actually wrote but it was enough to cause the religious elite to depart, the eldest departing first. As you will have noticed about this story, there are facts that we do not know. Some might find this unusual but John does state the primary reason for writing his Gospel, '...these are written down so that you may believe that Jesus is the Christ, the Son of God.' John 20:31.

John did not write to fill our heads with facts. He wrote to point our hearts to Jesus. The religious elite had no time for Jesus. He had only critical words for them as He saw through their façade and denounced them as hypocrites. He willingly preached to those the religious elite classed as 'sinners.'

There is a definite link between religion and pride. The law teachers and the Pharisees associated with those who claimed to be devout. Those who made no such claims listened to Jesus. Experience teaches that little has changed. Many devout people are still too interested in their religious observances to have time for Jesus and God's Salvation.

John tells us about a woman that was caught in the act of adultery. She, but not the adulterous man, was brought by the religious elite to Jesus. When they questioned Him, they misquoted the Law relating to adultery. They also failed to mention the legal evidence required both to prove the woman's guilt and to stone her to death. The Law stated:

- Leviticus 20:10 ERV. 'If a man has sexual relations with his neighbor's wife, both the man and the woman are guilty of adultery and must be put to death!'
- Deuteronomy 17:6-7. 'The witness of two or three people is required to put someone to death...

- Deuteronomy 19:15. ‘Suppose someone is charged with committing a crime of any kind. Then one witness won't be enough to prove he is guilty…’

Jesus gave one verbal and two written answers to the religious elite. We only know Jesus’ verbal answer. Adultery is one of many sins referred to in the Law so Jesus challenged them about their own sins. Beneath outward piety exists inherent sin. Religion and religious observances cannot eradicate it. Only Jesus’ death can eradicate sin.

We do not know what Jesus wrote. We know that He wrote:

- Twice.
- With His finger.
- On the ground.

Jesus wrote twice with His finger, as God did when He gave the Law to Moses. Maybe it was the Law that Jesus wrote twice with His finger on the ground.

- God gave His Law to ‘shut every mouth.’ So it comes as no surprise that when the religious elite saw what Jesus had written, they had nothing further to say and they departed. We are not told the reason for their orderly exit.
- Some teach that the older men would have committed more sins than the younger men but that would have required these self-righteous hypocrites considering that they were sinners, something they would be loath to do.
- The older men would be very experienced in the Law. Did they realise that they had not discredited Jesus by their subtle question and there was no point in staying further?

So-called religious people have always used the Bible for their own purposes. Read the Bible for yourself. Read verses in their context. It will save you from many doctrinal errors.

We have read about Jesus, the Son of God, dealing with a sinful woman and her accusers who claimed to be religious. He saw through their outward piety. He knew that He was dealing with sinful men. They considered themselves better than others but they sank as low as to misinterpret the Law they were supposed to uphold and teach in their efforts to trick Jesus. What Jesus said to them about their own sin and what He wrote on the ground was sufficient to end that particular encounter. But they, and others like them, would return with other trick questions because no matter what Jesus did or said, they thought He was only a man.

We know what Jesus said to the woman so we know how He dealt with God's Law and her sin. He asked her two questions. Although not immediately obvious, they both relate to the Law:

- "Where are they?"
- "Hasn't anyone found you guilty?"

In the absence of any witnesses, the Law stated that the woman could not be found guilty of adultery and could not be put to death. So Jesus said, "I don't find you guilty either." If an accused person is not found guilty under the Law because of lack of evidence, it does not mean that they have not sinned or that God will ignore what they have done. So Jesus told the woman to leave her life of sin.

"Leave Your Life of Sin"

Jesus' words prove that biblical repentance is turning your back upon your sin. Saying "sorry," or "I have sinned," without an intention to stop sinning might be how many are taught from the pulpit to seek forgiveness today but as we can see from the above story, simply saying sorry to God for past sins is not what God requires. God requires us to repent and that means a total change of lifestyle.

Jesus' words, "leave your life of sin," are not:

- difficult to understand.
- ambiguous.

Jesus told the woman to:

- stop committing adultery.
- change her lifestyle.

We have mentioned it already but we need to be as clear as possible about two particular problems that can particularly affect churchgoers who need to be aware of them:

- Repetition of words such as, 'I have sinned,' or 'I am a

sinner,' has no spiritual value. If we are sorry for our sins, we will stop sinning and accept Jesus as our Saviour and Lord. Words without repentance do not count with God.

- 'The Lord's Prayer' was Jesus' answer to a request, 'Lord, teach us to pray.' It does not provide God's forgiveness to all who say it. Its opening two words, 'Our Father,' tell us that it can only teach to pray those who:
    - Are already converted.
    - Have already repented.
    - Have already turned their backs on sin.
    - Are ashamed of their past life.

The above story of the adulterous woman also shows Jesus' attitude to those who trust in their religion and religious observances. Before moving on, we must refer to what Jesus said to them on a later occasion. '...the chief priests and the elders of the people came to him. "By what authority are you doing these things?" they asked...Jesus replied, "I will also ask you one question. If you answer me, I will tell you by what authority I am doing these things. Where did John's baptism come from? Was it from heaven? Or did it come from men?" They talked to each other about it. They said, "If we say, 'From heaven,' he will ask, "Then why didn't you believe him?" But what if we say, 'From men'? We are afraid of the people. Everyone believes that John was a prophet." So they answered Jesus, "We don't know." Jesus said, "Then I won't tell you by what authority I am doing these things either." Matthew 21:23-27.

As we can tell from both stories, the religious elite were clever and worldly wise enough to know when it was in their best interests to depart, or stay and say nothing. But they were not wise enough to recognise who Jesus was. Their religion and religious observances had blinded them to that vital truth. Whether you are religious or not each one of us must choose whether to accept or reject Jesus. But be assured that Heaven is for those who choose to accept Jesus as their Saviour and Lord. Those in the story above who did not accept that Jesus was the Son of God were the educated religious elite, the teachers and the administrators.

Why did Jesus say so very little to them or stop talking to them? Those who challenged Him did not intend to admit that they were sinners and repent. God has given each of us a free will. Many things have changed down the centuries but your right to choose your own eternal destiny has not. Always as now, you can choose to:

- ❖ Rely on Jesus for Heaven or try to get there your way.
- ❖ Admit or deny that you are a sinner who needs a Saviour.
- ❖ Repent of your sin or keep on sinning.
- ❖ Repent and change your lifestyle or retain your lifestyle.

We can tell from how Jesus dealt with religious, educated and high-ranking people that God has no respect for our religion, education or status. They only matter to men.

The above quotation is from Matthew's Gospel. Before Matthew, a Jew, met Jesus and was saved, he worked for the Romans as a tax collector. Unsurprisingly, tax collecting traitors were hated by the Jews. But, like Matthew, they could repent and be saved. Could they remain as tax collectors? Certainly not! Matthew's new life evidenced his Salvation.

Prior to Jesus' ministry John the Baptist preached, "Repent and believe the Gospel." For a time, although in different places, Jesus and John the Baptist preached this message. The religious elite ignored it but not those that they despised and classified as 'sinners.' Consider Jesus' words to the religious elite about John the Baptist's Gospel message, "'...you did not believe him. But the tax collectors and the prostitutes did. You saw this. But even then you did not turn away from your sins and believe him.'" Matthew 21: 32.

John the Baptist:

- ❖ He was sent by God to introduce Jesus to the Jewish Nation. His ministry is prophesied in the Old Testament.
- ❖ He identified himself to the religious elite. They ignored him and his message, "Repent and believe the Gospel."

The Religious Elite:

What Jesus said to them is as sad now as it was then. It still applies today. The religious elite had proof of what John the

Baptist's Gospel message could do as the tax collecting traitors and the prostitutes heard it and were saved. But those who are religious never seem to think about themselves as sinners who need to be saved and two thousand years have not changed religious people's attitude to the Gospel.

"You Saw This"

Jesus' words to the religious deserve our unhurried attention. We ask three vital and incisive questions that those who consider themselves to be religious should consider:

Question 1: Why were Jesus' words so damning against the religious? Answer: Look at the facts. Jesus said that the tax collectors and the prostitutes heard the Gospel and:

- Repented.
- Believed the Gospel.
- Stopped sinning.

Jesus said that those who were religious:

- Saw this change but ignored what they saw and continued to put faith in and follow their religion.
- Closed their eyes to the fact that the Gospel changes the lives of those who believe it.
- Did not reconsider their stubborn and prejudiced attitude to the Gospel.
- Hung onto their religion and religious procedures even though they had never changed a single life.

Question 2: Is it your religion and religious observances that prevents you from seeing that the Gospel changes lives?

Question 3: Is it your religious pride that prevents you from accepting the Gospel that is saving and changing others?

A Word of Caution: A Contrast

Repenting and believing that Gospel must be contrasted with reformation, moral improvement and concepts like turning over a new leaf and New Year's Resolutions. The contrast is obvious when you consider that the Gospel is divine. Reformation and the like are based solely on human effort.

- The Gospel is the 'Gospel of God.' It concerns Jesus and His willingness to save sinners. God sent Jesus to be the Saviour of the world. Those who believe the Gospel willingly repent and accept Jesus as Saviour and Lord.
- Human effort to make us better people to live with might be successful but it cannot deal with our sin problem. It cannot obtain forgiveness for the sins that are part and parcel of our everyday life. Only by repenting and believing the Gospel can we obtain forgiveness.
- Only when we accept that we are sinners and totally rely on what Jesus did for us will God declare us righteous or 'right with Him' and be our Heavenly Father.

Human Efforts

Do we know what God thinks about the good things that we do and our efforts to improve ourselves? We do but you are unlikely to hear it from many pulpits. It is anything but laudable and it would empty churches faster than fire alarms. Old Testament prophets spoke God's truth. They are contrasted with those called, 'false prophets.' Many of their ilk preach today. In Isaiah 64 Isaiah is speaking to God. The Jewish Nation that Isaiah belonged to was in poor spiritual health. The people lived as though God did not exist. If you recognise that Isaiah's words are a valid description of the times we live in, then time spent considering them is worthwhile. He wrote, So how can we be saved? All of us have become like someone who is 'unclean.' All of the good things we do are like polluted rags to you. All of us are like leaves that have dried up. Our sins sweep us away like the wind. No one prays to you. No one asks you for help. You have turned your face away from us. You have let us waste away because we have sinned so much.' Isaiah 64:5-7.

Isaiah's words, 'All of the good things we do are like polluted rags to you,' tell us what God thinks about our best efforts. As what God thinks about the best that we can do is so contrary to our own opinions, we quote how The Good News Bible and GOD'S WORD translate Isaiah 64:6 into English:

GNB: 'All of us have been sinful; even our best actions are filthy through and through. Because of our sins we are like leaves that wither and are blown away by the wind.'

GW: 'We've all become unclean, and all our righteous acts are like permanently stained rags. All of us shrivel like leaves, and our sins carry us away like the wind.'

Only when we see ourselves as a holy God sees us we will start to realise just how sinful we are. And only when the reality of our sin dawns on us will we ask Isaiah's question, "...how can we be saved?" Isaiah 64:5.

Isaiah foretold the coming of John the Baptist and Jesus and wrote about Jesus' crucifixion, burial and resurrection. Isaiah tells us that God placed on Jesus the sins of us all. We cannot comment in detail on Isaiah's knowledge of what Jesus would achieve on behalf of sinners when He died but we must quote an extract from Isaiah 53:11. God is speaking about Jesus whom He calls, "my godly servant." Consider God's words carefully. '"...My godly servant will make many people godly because of what he will accomplish. He will be punished for their sins."'

Many sincerely believe that their religion or their best efforts to be good people and the like will count favourably with God and they will be in Heaven. We have read various parts of the Bible that state that only those who repent and accept Jesus as Saviour and Lord will have their sins forgiven and be in Heaven. Isaiah 53:11 proves that if you are relying on your own efforts to obtain God's forgiveness and a place in Heaven, you are on what Jesus called, 'the broad road to destruction.' We consider Heaven in more detail later but mention one verse now. Revelation 21:27 says that only what is pure will enter it. This will not surprise many. We need to ask questions about the teaching in both Isaiah 53:11 and Revelation 21:27.

Question 1: Will those who are ungodly enter Heaven? Answer: 'Only what is pure will enter it.' Revelation 21:27.

Question 2: Will you be in Heaven? Answer: If "yes," we have another question for you.

Question 3: Did you make yourself godly? Answer: If you answered, "yes" as you believe that your life and efforts to please God are good enough, we have a further question.

Question 4: Are you as godly as Jesus? Answer: We would

be surprised if anybody answered that by their own efforts they had made themselves as godly as Jesus but only those as godly as Jesus will be in Heaven. God tells us how you can become as godly as Jesus. We repeat Isaiah 53:11 that we referred to above. God says, '"My godly servant will make many people godly because of what he will accomplish. He will be punished for their sins."'

- ❖ Because none of us were godly enough to enter Heaven, God points us to Jesus and what He has done for us. God wants you to know that His godly Son Jesus died on the cross to make you as godly as Himself.
- ❖ Grasp the truth that no matter how hard you try to live a good life, you will not achieve what Jesus' death has already accomplished for those who are saved.
- ❖ No one will get the benefit of Jesus' death unless they:
  - ❖ **Stop** trying to be good enough for God.
  - ❖ **Start** trusting in what Jesus has already achieved.

Revelation 21:27 states that only those whose names are written in the Lamb's Book of Life will enter Heaven.

The Book of Life

Before we comment on this special book, we consolidate what we have learnt. A song from our Sunday School days assists us in this task as it speaks so well of Jesus and what He has done for us. Two words in the chorus make it very personal. When you have read it we ask questions.

'He did not come to judge the world. He did not come to blame; He did not only come to seek, It was to save He came.

And **when** we call Him Saviour, And when **we** call Him Saviour, And when we call Him Saviour, Then we call Him by His name.'

Question 1: Has there been a time **when** you:

- ❖ Realised that because Jesus had died for your sins you needed Him to save you from your problem of sin?
- ❖ Asked God for 'a clean sheet,' as you were repenting of your sin and turning your back on your old way of life?
- ❖ Asked Jesus to be your personal Saviour?

Question 2: Does '**we**' include you?

- Do you often thank Jesus for being your Saviour?
- When you hear the Name 'Jesus,' does your heart immediately acknowledge Him as your Saviour and Lord?

Question 3: If we are totally frank about Jesus:

- Has Jesus little or no importance in your life?
- Are you relying on yourself for forgiveness and Heaven?
- Is this world with all its allurements more attractive than the assurance of forgiveness and a home in Heaven?
- Are you one of the many that hope that God will ignore your sin and let you enter Heaven?

Question 4: Do you think that a holy God will ignore your sin and permit you to enter Heaven because:

- Water was put on your head and words from a prayer book were read when you were a baby?
- At your funeral there will be a crucifix or incense on your coffin and prayers will be said from a prayer book?

So many must assume that:

- God does not know what lip service and hypocrisy is.
- Funeral services impress God.

We book holidays in advance. We want our names to be on the passenger list and the hotel to expect us. We do all that is necessary because we know that if our names are not on the various lists, it means no flight, no hotel and no holiday. So why do so many take a chance on their eternity when their names could be written in Heaven? They could know that all God's blessings are theirs for eternity. The title of this book, 'Is Your Name in the Book of Life,' was chosen to get you thinking about Heaven especially as some might not have known that their names could be written in Heaven.

- Jesus said to His disciples, '"...be glad that your names are written in heaven."' Luke 10: 20.
- Paul refers to his companions in his letter to Philippi, 'those who have worked together with me. Their names are all written in the Book of Life.' Philippians 4:3.

Jesus' disciples and Paul's companions had every reason to be glad that their names were written in the Book of Life. You will understand why from Revelation 20. 'Death and Hell were thrown into the lake of fire...Anyone whose name was not written in the Book of Life was thrown into the lake of fire.' Revelation 20:14-15.

Many refer to the Lake of Fire as 'Hell' and we have done the same in this book to save confusion. But the final punishment for those who reject Jesus is the Lake of Fire. There is far more in the Bible about this than we can comment on but we must refer to Revelation 21:27. The final words of the verse read, 'Only those whose names are written in the Lamb's Book of Life will enter the city.' Revelation 21:27. John wrote Revelation in the first person because he was personally given details of Heaven and the future. He saw Jesus in all His glory and majesty. Jesus said to him: '"...I am the Living One. I was dead. But look! I am alive for ever and ever! And I hold the keys to Death and Hell. So write down what you have seen. Write about what is happening now and what will happen later."' Revelation 1:18-19.

Revelation and other parts of the Bible contain imagery. We must understand this picture language to grasp the meaning of the text. Pharaoh's dream about the famine in Egypt is a good example. Joseph interpreted Pharaoh's dream about seven cows. Joseph said to Pharaoh, "the seven cows are seven years." In Revelation, we read about 'seven stars,' 'seven golden lampstands' and 'the sharp sword that has two edges.' We mention imagery because in Revelation 21:27 the Book of Life is called, 'The Lamb's Book of Life.' We know the 'Lamb' is Jesus because in John's Gospel we read in John 1:29 that John the Baptist identified Jesus as the 'Lamb of God.' 'The next day John saw Jesus coming toward him. John said, "Look! The Lamb of God! He takes away the sin of the world!"' We are not told why John the Baptist chose this special Name for Jesus but he knew the Old Testament. It contains many references to lambs and sacrifices e.g.

- Abraham: 'Abraham said, "God himself will provide the lamb for the burnt offering, my son?"' Genesis 22:8.
- The Passover lamb: 'Each family must kill a Passover lamb.' Exodus 12:21.

- The redemption of the firstborn son: 'Sacrifice a lamb to buy back…every oldest son.' Exodus 34:20.
- The sin offering lamb: 'Suppose he brings a lamb as his sin offering…It must not have any flaws.' Leviticus 4:32.
- The daily Temple sacrifice: 'Every day you must provide a lamb that is a year old. It must not have any flaws. It is a burnt offering to me.' Ezekiel 46:13.

The Lamb of Isaiah 53? We have already quoted these verses but time spent musing on them will be time well spent. '…the servant was pierced because we had sinned. He was crushed because we had done what was evil. He was punished to make us whole again. His wounds have healed us. All of us are like sheep. We have wandered away from God. All of us have turned to our own way. And the LORD has placed on his servant the sins of all of us. He was beaten down and made to suffer. But he didn't open his mouth. He was led away like a sheep to be killed. Lambs are silent while their wool is being cut off. In the same way, he didn't open his mouth.' Isaiah 53:5-7.

Isaiah's Imagery

God's Servant is Jesus. He was 'pierced because we had sinned. He was crushed because we had done what was evil.' Sheep are mentioned twice:

- The first time, they are a picture of us.
- The second time, they are a picture of Jesus.

Question 1: Why are all of us like sheep? Answer: We have an inbuilt bent to wander. Isaiah does not refer to some of us, he writes, 'all of us.' All of us have wandered away from God.

Question 2: Why have we all wandered away from God? Answer: Isaiah is blunt. We all prefer our own way to God's way. So he adds, 'All of us have turned to our own way.'

Question 3: What is wrong with 'our own way?' Answer: It is the sinful way.

Isaiah states that 'the Lord has placed on his servant the sins of all of us.' So we can tell you without hesitation or doubt that anybody anywhere can be saved because Jesus died for the 'sins of us all.' But do not take those words out of their context and claim that if Jesus died for us all, then all are saved. Three verses in Isaiah 53 prove that would be wrong:

Isaiah 53:1. 'Who has believed?' There would be no need for anyone to believe if all were saved. It is foolish to think that God will treat believer and unbeliever alike.

Isaiah 53:3. 'They didn't accept him.' It is foolish to think that God will treat those who reject Jesus in the same way as those who accept Jesus.

Isaiah 53:11. '...many people godly...' 'Many' is not 'all.' All will not be made godly. If Isaiah had meant 'everyone' he would have written it in clear terms. When he meant everyone, he had no difficulty in writing, 'all we like sheep have gone astray,' and 'the Lord has placed on his servant the sins of us all.' Isaiah intended to make a contrast between believers and unbelievers. Do not be misled by those who fail to make this contrast and who preach that we are all going to Heaven 'our own way.' Isaiah tells us that 'our own way' is not God's way.

Jesus was Led Away Like a Sheep to be Killed

Sheep do not resist when they are taken to be killed. Jesus was led away like a sheep to be killed. His death was voluntary. The time and the place of His birth and death were foretold centuries before. He offered no resistance to those instructed to kill Him. In John 10:17 we read what He said before the Jews began to plot His death. '"The reason my Father loves me is that I give up my life. But I will take it back again. No one takes it from me. I give it up myself."'

Jesus was as Silent as a Lamb

Isaiah states that Jesus would suffer intense cruelty without complaint. He would be as silent as a lamb being shorn. But no study of Jesus as the Lamb of God would be complete without the story of an Ethiopian mentioned in Acts 8 and Peter's reference to Jesus as the perfect lamb in 1 Peter.

The Lamb of God and the Ethiopian Official

An Ethiopian was returning home reading from Isaiah 53. He wanted to know to whom Isaiah referred. Philip explained to him that Isaiah was referring to Jesus. We read,'Here is the part of Scripture the official was reading. It says, He was led like a sheep to be killed. Just as lambs are silent while their wool is being cut off, he did not open his mouth...Then Philip began with that same part of Scripture. He told him the good news about Jesus.' Extract from Acts 8:32-35.

1 Peter: Jesus, the Lamb of God

Peter was one of Jesus' apostles. He spent over three years with Jesus and he refers to Him as a lamb. Peter did not write to everyone. He only wrote to believers. We know that because of the way that he describes their relationship to Jesus, their salvation and their faith in 1 Peter 1:7-12. Peter writes, 'Your troubles have come in order to prove that your faith is real. It is worth more than gold. Gold can pass away even though fire has made it pure. Your faith is meant to bring praise, honor and glory to God. That will happen when Jesus Christ returns. Even though you have not seen him, you love him. Though you do not see him now, you believe in him. You are filled with a glorious joy that can't be put into words. You are receiving the salvation of your souls. It is the result of your faith. The prophets searched very hard and with great care to find out about that salvation. They spoke about the grace that was going to come to you. They wanted to find out when that salvation would come. The Spirit of Christ in them was telling them about the sufferings of Christ that were going to come. He was also telling them about the glory that would follow. It was made known to the prophets that they were not serving themselves. Instead, they were serving you when they spoke about the things that you have now heard. Those who have preached the good news to you have told you those things. They have done it with the help of the Holy Spirit sent from heaven.'

What Peter wrote merits unhurried attention. It needs to be preached and emphasised as many seem to be unaware of it. He had more experience than most in spiritual matters. We briefly consider matters that relate to the Gospel:

- Our personal response to the Gospel.
- The Old Testament prophets and the Gospel
- The grace coming to us.
- Those who preach the Gospel.

Our Personal Response to the Gospel

- 'To prove that your faith is real.' If your faith was tested today, would it prove false?
- 'You believe in him.' Have you a personal faith in Jesus? Could it be that in reality you only know facts about Him?
- 'You are filled with a glorious joy that can't be put into words.' If you are not filled with this glorious joy, you must ask yourself whether your faith in Jesus is false.
- 'The salvation of your souls.' There is a contrast between Salvation and moral improvement. Contrary to what is being preached today in many pulpits, Jesus did not come to make us better people. He came to save our souls from sin and Hell. When we are saved, the Holy Spirit will teach us how to live holy lives.
- 'The result of your faith.' Peter states that our faith results in our Salvation. He mentions nothing else that results in our Salvation. If you are trusting in your good deeds for Salvation, you, and those like you will remain unsaved.

The Old Testament Prophets and the Gospel

The prophets wanted to know more about the future events they wrote about. Because the birth, life, death, resurrection and glorification of Jesus are now historical events, even though the prophets did not fully understand what they wrote, we can see the accuracy of their prophecies and use both the Old and the New Testaments to preach the Gospel.

Before we look at three matters that are linked by the word 'come,' it is vital that we note that the phrases, 'that salvation,' and 'the sufferings of Christ' are inseparable:

- There could be no Salvation without 'the sufferings of Christ.' If Jesus had not died for our sins, there would have been no Gospel and no Salvation for sinners.
- Be wary of any who purport to preach the Gospel but do not mention that Jesus suffered and died so that God could offer His Salvation to sinners.

'The grace that was going to come to you.'

'Grace' is 'divine blessing.' The prophets only knew that it was coming. They only had limited information about:

- ‘when that salvation would come.’
- ‘the sufferings of Christ that were going to come.’

We cannot quote all the verses linking these events. But we must quote what Peter said when he defended himself and John after they had been arrested for preaching the Gospel in the Temple grounds after a lame man had been healed. “‘...You nailed Jesus Christ of Nazareth to the cross. But God raised him from the dead. It is through Jesus’ name that this man stands healed in front of you...You can't be saved by believing in anyone else. God has given us no other name under heaven that will save us.’ Extract from Acts 4:10-12.

Peter referred to Jesus’ death and made two emphatic statements that many today seem loath to accept. He said,

- “You can't be saved by believing in anyone else.”
- “God has given us no other name...that will save us.”

There are many religious people today who have the highest regard for Peter and yet experience teaches that they are not familiar with what he said about Jesus and God’s Salvation.

‘Those Who Preach the Gospel’

The Gospel is God’s Good News. Some might question this and think that we have overlooked that we have written that:

- God will judge unforgiven sinners.
- The Bible teaches that the majority will not be saved.

We reaffirm that the Gospel is God’s Good News. Those who want their sins forgiven can repent and believe the Gospel. They will avoid God’s judgment for their sins and receive all God’s eternal blessings.

‘A glorious joy that can’t be put into words.’

How did Peter describe the joy that God gives to believers? He said, ‘You are filled with a glorious joy that can’t be put into words.’ But he never pretended that a believer’s life was easy, or that they would be healthy and wealthy. To give you a view of real Christianity, we quote the first six verses of 1 Peter. ‘I, Peter, am writing this letter. I am an apostle of

Jesus Christ. I am sending this letter to you, God's chosen people. You are strangers in the world. You are scattered all over Pontus, Galatia, Cappadocia, Asia and Bithynia. You have been chosen in keeping with what God the Father had planned. That happened through the Spirit's work to make you pure and holy. God chose you so that you might obey Jesus Christ. He wanted you to be made clean by the blood of Christ. May more and more grace and peace be given to you. Give praise to the God and Father of our Lord Jesus Christ. In his great mercy he has given us a new birth and a hope that is alive. It is alive because Jesus Christ rose from the dead. He has given us new birth so that we might share in what belongs to him. It is a gift that can never be destroyed. It can never spoil or even fade away. It is kept in heaven for you. Through faith you are kept safe by God's power. Your salvation is going to be completed. It is ready to be shown to you in the last days. Because you know this, you have great joy. You have joy even though you may have had to suffer for a little while. You may have had to suffer sadness in all kinds of trouble.' 1 Peter 1:1-6. Peter states that we can be:

- Pure and holy, made clean by the blood of Christ.
- Kept safe by God's power.

Peter states that we can have:

- Grace, peace, mercy, a new birth and a hope that is alive.
- A share of Jesus' inheritance reserved in Heaven.
- A salvation that is going to be completed in the last days.
- Great joy.

In view of all God's blessings for any who are willing to repent and believe the Gospel, are you surprised that we have reaffirmed that the Gospel is God's Good News?

The Gospel, the Holy Spirit and the Prophets

There is a matter concerning the Gospel that we could easily miss on a cursory reading of 1 Peter. Peter mentions that the Gospel has come to us by:

- Divine involvement: the Holy Spirit.
- Human involvement: the Prophets.

The Holy Spirit told the prophets about Christ's future sufferings and glory and that they were writing for the future and not their own time. Today Gospel preachers refer to historical events that link with and substantiate what the prophets foretold. Although Gospel preachers are human, they, like the prophets have the Holy Spirit's guidance and support. Studying these truths will assist our evangelism. Peter writes the truths he learnt from both Jesus and his personal experience. The Gospels and Acts record the lessons he learnt. What he wrote applies to all who talk or write about the Gospel. It is not exclusively for evangelists or those who preach. It applies equally to those who talk to family and friends. It is the Gospel message itself, not how or where it is delivered, that counts.

The Gospel: A Summary

- The Holy Spirit was in the prophets telling them about 'the sufferings of Christ and the glory that would follow.'
- The Holy Spirit has been sent from Heaven. He will guide and assist those who preach the Gospel.
- The divine and the human must combine. Nothing less will result in the 'Salvation of souls.'
- When you have preached the Gospel, you have done all that you can do. It is then the work of the Holy Spirit to introduce unbelievers to Jesus the Saviour.
- Humans cannot do the exclusive work of the Holy Spirit.

The Gospel and Your Responsibility

Your responsibility to God is to 'preach the Gospel.' Arguments about religion, if the Bible contains contradictions, myths and the like will not result in the 'Salvation of souls.' If you win every argument, that is all you will achieve:

- The essential part of the Gospel is, 'the sufferings of Christ and the glory that would follow.'
- You can preach and not mention 'the sufferings of Christ and the glory that would follow,' but you cannot preach the Gospel without mentioning these essentials truths.
- As we will read later, those who do not preach the true Gospel preach a 'different Gospel.'

So how many are preaching a 'different Gospel' today? Some are reluctant to refer to sin and God's judgment. Many would prefer to refer only to God's love and John 3:16 instinctively comes to mind. 'For God so loved the world that he gave his one and only Son, that whoever believes in him shall not perish but have eternal life.'

- Can you preach 'God's love' and omit 'shall not perish' without being unfaithful to God and to the unsaved?
- Can you preach 'eternal life' and omit 'eternal death?'

Peter states that the Gospel refers to the sufferings of Christ. Gospel preachers must preach why it was necessary for 'Christ to suffer.' Jesus said, '"Did not the Messiah have to suffer these things and then enter his glory?"' Luke 24:26. If you do not refer to these 'essentials of the Gospel' you are unfaithful and you preach a false Gospel. In 1 Corinthians 15:1-4 Paul wrote, 'I want to remind you of the good news I preached to you. You received it and have put your faith in it. Because you believed the good news, you are saved. But you must hold firmly to the message I preached to you. If you don't, you have believed it for nothing. What I received I passed on to you. And it is the most important of all. Here is what it is. Christ died for our sins, just as Scripture said he would. He was buried. He was raised from the dead on the third day, just as Scripture said he would be.'

Paul, the Gospel, and Corinth. 1 Corinthians 15.

Paul preached the Gospel in Corinth and those who believed it formed a local church. A cursory reading of 1 Corinthians 15:1-4 might not indicate that there was a serious problem at Corinth. Preachers can innocently imply that Paul only wrote to set out the essentials of the Gospel. But if we probe the verses we become aware that the Gospel was under attack.

Paul's Four Statements about the Gospel

- You received it and have put your faith in it.
- Because you believed the good news, you are saved.
- You must hold firmly to the message I preached to you. If you don't, you have believed it for nothing.
- What I received I passed on to you.

The Gospel: The Problem

Paul thought that all the people in the Corinthian church had received the Gospel he preached and had put their faith in it.

- But humans cannot see the divine transaction that occurs when a sinner repents and believes the Gospel.
- A change of lifestyle is the only visible evidence of the divine transaction that involves the Holy Spirit and saves.

No one knew this better than Paul. The disciples in Jerusalem had good reason to suspect that his conversion was not genuine and they had to decide whether or not to admit him to their fellowship. They ascertained from Barnabas that Paul had not only believed the Gospel, he had preached it and had risked his life doing so. It was only when the disciples learnt of the change in Paul's life that he was accepted into their fellowship.

Only genuine believers hold fast to the Gospel. This comes as no surprise because it is only by believing the Gospel that sinners are saved and indwelt by the Holy Spirit. Experience teaches that genuine believers have:

- An indescribable joy.
- A desire to see others saved.
- No desire to revert to being unbelievers.

The Gospel had 'the usual outcome' in Corinth. For two thousand years, wherever the Gospel is preached:

- Some, but not all, are willing to listen to it.
- Some, but not all, believe it.
- Some, but not all, are saved.

It seems that some in Corinth wrongly thought that they were saved. How this tragedy occurred and what they had believed we are not told but it was not the Gospel. So to deal with this problem Paul put into writing various historical and scriptural facts. Together they are the essential content of the Gospel. Those who attended the church at Corinth could read these facts and check if they believed them.

- Genuine believers would believe every fact.
- Any who did not believe every fact had 'believed in vain.'

But no one could 'pick and choose' what facts they believed and those who preached at Corinth could check if they were preaching 'a different Gospel' because those who:

- ❖ Omitted any of these facts did not preach the Gospel.
- ❖ Added to these facts did not preach the Gospel.

Those who heard preachers who 'omitted or added' to these facts had been misled and could not have been saved.

The Relevance of the Old Testament to the Gospel

Paul in 1 Corinthians 15 and Peter in 1 Peter 1 refer to the Old Testament to confirm the facts of the Gospel. This shows the relevance to the Gospel of the prophecies about 'the sufferings of Christ and the glory that should follow'. Paul received a direct revelation about the Gospel. That is why in 1 Corinthians 15:3 he wrote that he passed on what he had received. He did not learn the Gospel from a human source:

- ❖ Paul knew that the Gospel he preached was authentic.
- ❖ Nothing was more important. Hence he wrote, 'And it is the most important of all.' 1 Corinthians 15:3.

Although Paul referred to the Old Testament to confirm the facts of the Gospel, he stressed the importance of what he was personally writing. Look at his references to himself:

- ❖ 'I want to remind you..,'
- ❖ 'I preached to you…'
- ❖ 'What I received I passed on to you…'

Paul put the Gospel he received and preached on the same divine status as the Old Testament.

Paul and the Gospel: The Problem at Galatia

It was not only at Corinth that there were problems with the Gospel. Men have always wanted to add or subtract from it. Read the Bible and then look at the churches today. You will see man's influence on Biblical doctrines and practices.

- ❖ Men changed what Jesus and the apostles taught relatively soon after they first heard it.
- ❖ The Bible is not silent as to the error that men wanted to bring into the Church even when the apostles were alive.

Read what Paul wrote about the changes the Galatians were making to the good news of the Gospel and note that:

- Paul links the Gospel with God.
- Paul equates changing the Gospel to deserting God.

Paul does not give the Galatians a 'gentle telling off' or say that they have been 'naughty.' As the Gospel was under attack, this was not the time for soft words. This was blistering criticism. 'I am amazed. You are so quickly deserting the One who chose you because of the grace that Christ has provided. You are turning to a different 'good news.' What you are accepting is really not the good news at all. It seems that some people have gotten you all mixed up. They are trying to twist the good news about Christ. But suppose even we should preach a different 'good news.' Suppose even an angel from heaven should preach it. I'm talking about a different one than the good news we gave you. Let anyone who does that be judged by God forever. I have already said it. Now I will say it again. Anyone who preaches a 'good news' that is different from the one you accepted should be judged by God forever. Am I now trying to get people to think well of me? Or do I want God to think well of me? Am I trying to please people? If I were, I would not be serving Christ. Brothers and sisters, here is what I want you to know. The good news I preached is not something a human being made up. No one gave it to me. No one taught it to me. Instead, I received it from Jesus Christ. He showed it to me.' Galatians 1:6-12.

Paul also identifies a real problem that affects some Christians' actions and some church's approach to evangelism. He wrote, 'Am I now trying to get people to think well of me? Am I trying to please people?' Galatians 1:10.

Experience teaches that over the years there have been those who have sincerely thought that unbelievers would find attending church and Christianity more attractive if various changes were made and new ideas introduced. Many among the present generation of Christians are saddened when they see their church almost empty and their supermarkets overcrowded on a Sunday. Some have sought solutions to the problems by 'A plan of action.' A 'public relations committee' has addressed local complaints such as car parking. 'Mother and Toddler' activities and the like have been setup. But some would like to make further changes because they consider it old fashioned to preach the Gospel in the 21st century. They disapprove of church services where the emphasis is on the Gospel being preached. They have similar views about preaching the Gospel in the open air. Some ask preachers to avoid references to sin and judgment. Family services are preferred to those which focus on the Gospel. Some churches do not now actively engage in evangelical witness.

Question: Is an evangelistic campaign every few years or an annual 'Alpha Course' enough to discharge each believer's obligation to 'go into all the world and preach the Gospel?

We live in a day of opinions. We only ask for opinions. We should ask for and question motives. In Galatians 1:10 we read Paul's motives for preaching the Gospel. We need to quote the full verse because the 'unbeliever friendly' and 'church best practice public relations' approaches to Gospel preaching mentioned above have consequences that we cannot ignore. Paul wrote, 'Am I now trying to get people to think well of me? Or do I want God to think well of me? Am I trying to please people? If I were, I would not be serving Christ.' Galatians 1:10.

- ❖ We cannot read Galatians 1:10 without noting the choices. As in most spiritual things, there are only two.
    - ❖ We choose God's way, or our way.
    - ❖ Anything that is not God's way is our way.

What about a compromise between God's way and our way? A compromise requires both sides to make concessions:

- ❖ What changes would you ask God to make?
- ❖ What concessions would you expect God to make?

Paul summed up what he had always preached everywhere and whatever the status, nationalities or the beliefs of those he preached to. In Acts 20:21 we read that he always preached, 'repentance toward God, and faith toward our Lord Jesus Christ.' As you will have noted, whether we consider the Gospel preaching of Jesus, John the Baptist, Peter or Paul, they emphasised that repentance precedes belief.

Sin and Repentance

The Gospel must start with sin and repentance. Those who are not prepared to preach sin and repentance ought not to:

- be regarded as Gospel preachers.
- claim that they preach the Gospel. What they preach is not, to quote Paul, 'the good news at all.'

Do not be surprised if no one is genuinely saved because only the true Gospel can save. And do not be surprised when those churches that have abandoned the true Gospel have the same problems as the churches of Corinth and Galatia.

1 Peter 1

We did not consider three matters in 1 Peter 1:12 before we switched our attention to 'Paul and the Gospel.' They are:

- '...they were serving you when they spoke about the things that you have now heard.'
- 'Those who have preached the good news to you have told you these things'
- 'They have done it with the help of the Holy Spirit sent from heaven.'

In considering these three matters, we need to merge Peter's teaching in 1 Peter with Paul's teaching in 1 Corinthians 15 and Galatians 1. We consider the first two matters together.

- Peter wrote, 'They were serving you when they spoke about the things that you have now heard.' 'Those who have preached the good news to you have told you these things.' 1 Peter 1:12. Peter refers to what the prophets wrote as 'the things that you have now heard.' Note the word, 'you' that Peter uses four times:
  - Serving **you**.
  - **You** have now heard.
  - Preached the good news to **you**.
  - Have told **you** these things.

Peter is not writing about something we have been told. He is writing about our personal experience of the Gospel. Two questions will highlight a problem that the Bible and experience teach is not uncommon.

Question 1: Are some who were saved when they believed the Gospel now preaching a different Gospel to unbelievers?

Question 2: Are some who were saved when they believed the Gospel now preaching a 'more acceptable version' of the Gospel to unbelievers?

The Answer to both questions is 'yes' and it should shock you. The problem concerns trust. It is not that God cannot be trusted. Not all believers can be trusted. Lack of trust is not a recent problem. Paul wrote about it. 'Pass on to men you can trust the things you've heard me say. Then they will be able to teach others also.' 2 Titus 2:2. Paul referred to 'men you can trust.' So Titus had to decide between believers he could trust and those he could not. Can we personally be trusted with the divine task of passing God's truth on to others without adding to it or subtracting from it?

The Holy Spirit and the Gospel

The Gospel is 'the Gospel of God.' God entrusts those who believe it to pass it on exactly as they received it. Believers are not without help to fulfil their obligations to God:

- The prophets were helped by the Holy Spirit, 'the Spirit of Christ,' to write about Christ's sufferings and His glory.
- The Holy Spirit helped the prophets write centuries before He came to permanently indwell believers.
- The Old Testament refers to the Holy Spirit but His involvement with men before Jesus ascended was only temporary. Peter noted that, those who preached the good news had the help of the Holy Spirit 'sent from Heaven.'
- The Holy Spirit has from the first Pentecost after Jesus' death, resurrection and ascension to Heaven indwelt believers on a permanent basis.

Do not underestimate or minimise the Holy Spirit's personal involvement in the preaching of the Gospel. The Holy Spirit:

- Assisted prophets to write the essentials of the Gospel.
- Assists those who preach the essentials of the Gospel.

Remember that when Jesus spoke about the new birth to Nicodemus He said, "It is the same with everyone who is born through the Spirit."

The Gospel and Faithfulness

For the sake of clarity you ought to know that believers are only required to be faithful in the way they preach the Gospel. Because the Salvation of unbelievers is a divine work, believers are not required to be successful. Jesus' well-known words were, "good and faithful servant." A good servant is a faithful servant. A servant only carries out the master's instructions. It is the servant's master who is responsible for everything.

- ❖ Question: Does the Holy Spirit help those who cannot be trusted, the preachers of a 'different Gospel?'
- ❖ Answer: Even a cursory reading of Galatians 1:1-6 and 2 Titus 2:2 indicates that the answer is 'no.'

'The priceless blood of Christ. He is a perfect lamb.'

Peter spent three years with Jesus and in 1 Peter 1:18-19 he refers to Jesus as 'a perfect lamb.' 'The blood of Christ set you free from an empty way of life. That way of life was handed down to you by your own people long ago. You know that you were not bought with things that can pass away, like silver or gold. Instead, you were bought by the priceless blood of Christ. He is a perfect lamb. He doesn't have any flaws at all.' 1 Peter 1:18-19.

Peter was writing to persecuted believers whose faith was being sorely tested. In troubled times we need to rely on something that endures. So Peter reminded them of the divine event that had changed their lives. They knew what he meant as he wrote, 'You know…' What did they know?

- ❖ They were no longer sin's slaves.
- ❖ They were like slaves that had been bought by a benefactor and set free.
- ❖ The price paid to set them free was 'the blood of Christ.'
- ❖ Jesus' blood was priceless as Jesus was 'a perfect lamb.'

Being religious and doing good deeds can mislead us into

thinking that we are good enough for God. Note how Peter contrasts the unbeliever's and the believer's 'way of life:'

- The unbeliever's life is 'an empty way of life that is handed down from generation to generation.'
- The believer's life has 'before and after' periods:
  - Before they were saved they were sin's slaves.
  - After they were saved they were set free.

What is 'an empty way of life?' Translators of the Bible had difficulty with these words. We quote three translations:

GNB: 'the worthless manner of life.'
GW: 'the worthless life.'
MSG: 'dead-end, empty-headed life.'

Peter was not being very complimentary about the lives of the unsaved. His words are not surprising as he had not only experienced a miraculous change in his own life, he had witnessed it in the lives of those who believed the Gospel.

We have either experienced this change or we have not. It would be difficult for anyone to disagree with Peter that unless we have been saved we follow the way of life that:

- everyone around us follows.
- is handed down from generation to generation.

Peter was only writing to believers whose sins were forgiven when they were saved so he does not refer to their sins. He just reminds them that they had a worthless way of life before they were saved. But he did not leave the matter there. They now had a divine eternal life that was worthwhile. They might be badly treated but nobody could take away their Salvation:

- They had been purchased from the slave market of sin. The purchase price was the priceless blood of Christ.
- They were sinners but a perfect Lamb a Lamb without flaws, had been sacrificed for their sins. Jesus' death for them had made it possible for God to forgive them.
- Their future was secure as the priceless blood of Christ was eternal. It could never be corrupted or destroyed.

Silver and gold is desired by those who see wealth as an

entrée to the fleeting pleasures of this world. Peter makes the contrast clear. The blood of Christ is not only priceless, it will last forever.

AN INTRODUCTION TO 'THE LAMB'S BOOK OF LIFE'

There are many references in the Bible to the 'Book of Life.' There is a hint in Revelation 13:8 that the Book's name might be changed to 'The Lamb's Book of Life.' Only in Revelation 21:27 do we actually read the full name of the book:

- Revelation 13:8. 'The Book of Life belongs to the Lamb…'
- Revelation 21:27. 'Only those whose names are written in the Lamb's Book of Life will enter the city.'

We need to consider the Book's new title in its context. John writes, 'I saw a new heaven and a new earth. The first heaven and the first earth were completely gone…I saw the Holy City, the new Jerusalem…I heard a loud voice from the throne. It said, "Now God makes his home with people. He will live with them. They will be his people. And God himself will be with them and be their God. He will wipe away every tear from their eyes. There will be no more death or sadness. There will be no more crying or pain. Things are no longer the way they used to be." He who was sitting on the throne said, "I am making everything new!" Then he said, "Write this down. You can trust these words. They are true." He said to me, "It is done. I am the Alpha and the Omega, the First and the Last. I am the Beginning and the End. Anyone who is thirsty may drink from the spring of the water of life. It doesn't cost anything! Anyone who overcomes will receive all this from me. I will be his God, and he will be my child. "But others will have their place in the lake of fire that burns with sulfur…It is the second death." …The Spirit took me to a huge, high mountain. He showed me Jerusalem, the Holy City. It was coming down out of heaven from God…The wall of the city had 12 foundations. Written on them were the names of the 12 apostles of the Lamb…The main street of the city was made out of pure gold, as clear as glass. I didn't see a temple in the city. This was because the Lamb and the Lord God who rules over all are its temple. The city does not need the sun or moon to shine on it. God's glory is its light, and the Lamb is its lamp…Only those whose names are written in the Lamb's Book of Life will enter the city.' Extract from Revelation 21.

John recalls what he saw and heard in his vision. He relates it in the same imagery that he saw. Lack of space means we cannot comment in detail but there are certain truths that we cannot ignore. We comment on these in the order that John wrote them as he gives us a brief picture of the believers' eternal future. There is little in the Bible about the place where believers will dwell eternally with God. There are words here and there but they are in very general terms. We know little more than that Heaven is a wonderful place and that God's blessings for believers are beyond anything that they could imagine. The Bible, and Jesus' teaching in The Gospels, give us more detail about Hell than Heaven. That should cause no surprise as the Gospel that Jesus preached, and we preach today, centres on what Jesus has done so that sinners can be forgiven and escape God's Judgment.

Many assume that life will always be the same. These verses teach us that the day will come when God will say, "I am making everything new!" A new creation is necessary because sin has contaminated and ruined this present one. Hence a day is coming when sin will be completely gone. Note that God speaks to and interacts with His people. In these verses we have a picture of God wiping tears from their eyes. Sadly, so many think of God as merciless and unsympathetic. They are quick to express their embittered feelings against God after natural disasters and similar incidents. But there is no consistency in the attitude of those who badmouth God. Some:

- See Him as the One who disapproves of their pleasures.
- Blame Him for everything that goes wrong.
- Refer to calamities and deny that He is a God of love.

But we can be certain of one thing. They will all continue to sin and refuse to repent and believe the Gospel.

We emphasise that God is a God who gives good gifts to His children. If you are willing to be saved, you will discover this for yourself. You will be indwelt by the Holy Spirit. He will replace your desire for sinful pleasures with a desire to be holy. You will then know the truth of Jesus words in Matthew 7:11, '"Even though you are evil, you know how to give good gifts to your children. How much more will your Father who is in heaven give good gifts to those who ask him!"' Many regard John 3:16 as the most concise 'Gospel Message' in the Bible. Note the emphasis that God is a God who gives. 'For God so loved the world that he gave his one and only Son, that whoever believes in him shall not perish but have eternal life.' God gave His only Son so that He might give you and all who believe in Jesus eternal life. You will note from Revelation 21:6-7 that in the future God is still giving:

- 'Anyone who is thirsty may drink from the spring of the water of life. It doesn't cost anything!' Revelation 21:6.
- 'Anyone who overcomes will receive all this from me. I will be his God, and he will be my child.' Revelation 21:7.

Question: Why do God's Salvation and the blessings that God wants to give you cost you nothing? Answer: Jesus paid the price for them when He shed His own blood. You recall how Peter explained this truth. 'The blood of Christ set you free from an empty way of life. That way of life was handed down to you by your own people long ago. You know that you were not bought with things that can pass away, like silver or gold. Instead, you were bought by the priceless blood of Christ.' Peter 1:18-19.

'Anyone who overcomes...I will be his God...'

What do we have to 'overcome?' John gives us the answer in the first of the three letters he wrote. It is variously translated in the Bibles in popular use. In 1 John 2:13 we read;

NIV: 'you have overcome the evil one.'

GNB: 'you have defeated the Evil One.'

GW: 'you have won the victory over the evil one.'

An overcomer is one who actively fights evil and wins. Believers must be 'on guard' against evil at all times because it will continually seek to 'overcome' them. Experience proves that the more effective believers are for God, the more Satan will seek to make them sin so that they become ineffective.

Although they are not referred to as 'overcomers' it seems appropriate to write about the Ephesian believers. They received Jesus' commendation because when problems beset them they triumphed over evil. In Revelation 2 we read that Jesus told John to write to them. Jesus said, "'I know what you are doing. You work long and hard. I know you can't put up with those who are evil. You have tested those who claim to be apostles but are not. You have found out that they are liars. You have been faithful and have put up with a lot of trouble because of me. You have not given up.'" Revelation 2:2-3. Jesus spoke to believers. They were not working 'long and hard' to obtain Salvation, they were already saved but Jesus knew that they had not given up. They had overcome evil.

'You Can't Put Up with Those Who are Evil'

The Bible and experience teach that believers will be targeted by Satan and those who do his bidding. Those recently saved will be particularly vulnerable. Regrettably, there are those who teach that the Christian life should be easier than it actually is. But Jesus knew what His followers could expect from this evil world and He included the words, 'deliver us from evil,' in the prayer He taught them to pray, often called, 'The Lord's Prayer. In John 17:1-26 we can read Jesus' personal prayer to His Father. It is worth studying. Jesus prays for His disciples. We only have space to consider two verses. "'I have given them your word. The world has hated them...they are not part of the world any more than I am. I do not pray that you will take them out of the world. I pray that you will keep them safe from the evil one.'" John 17:14-15.

'The world has hated them.' John 17:14.

Why did Jesus refer to the world's hatred? Consider the divine transaction that occurs when a sinner is saved. That is the moment when a sinner repents and believes the Gospel.

- Repentance involves a lifestyle change so repentant sinners turn their back on their old way of life.
- Unrepentant sinners please themselves how they live but repentant sinners live to please God.

A believer's lifestyle change will be seen by their unbelieving family and friends who belong to this world. Believers belong to Jesus and He said why they would be hated, '"...they are not part of the world any more than I am."' John 17:14.

Jesus did not exaggerate. If He had meant to say that the world will 'misunderstand' or 'dislike' believers He would have said so. 'Hated' means 'detested.' Sadly experience teaches that some believers go out of their way to be hated thinking it is a sign of their spirituality. In reality they receive the same response as all who behave badly. Their aggressive style of preaching and their 'know all' attitude to spiritual questions and problems encourages people to avoid them like the plague. They are bad advertisements for Christ and Christianity. Unfortunately, their bad attitude to unbelievers also tends to be their attitude to believers.

Completely good, right and true: The Ephesian Believers

We read what Jesus said about the Ephesians. Paul had already written to them about the things that are 'completely good, right and true.' It seems from Revelation 2 that the Ephesians had taken Paul's words to heart. 'Don't let anyone fool you with words that don't mean anything. Because of things like that, God is angry with those who don't obey. So don't go along with people like that. At one time you were in the dark. But now you are in the light because of what the Lord has done. Live like children of the light. The light produces what is completely good, right and true. Find out what pleases the Lord. Have nothing to do with the acts of darkness. They don't produce anything good. Show what they are really like. It is shameful even to talk about what people who don't obey do in secret. But everything the light shines on can be seen.' Ephesians 5:6-13. The Ephesian believers were proactive in avoiding evil. They are praised by Jesus for this. They must have made personal decisions about the company they chose to keep because they avoided 'those who are evil.' The tests are clearly stated:

- If it is not 'completely good, right and true,' it is evil.
- If it does not 'please the Lord,' it is evil.

Question: Would Jesus have praised the believers at Ephesus if they had been arrogant, aggressive and haughty when dealing with 'those who are evil?' Answer: No. Paul emphasises that 'The light produces what is completely good, right and true.' Arrogance, aggression, haughtiness and the like are not produced by 'what the Lord has done' for believers. They are a part of the darkness that does not 'produce anything good.'

'You have tested those who claim to be apostles…'

Shortly after the Christian Church began, false teachers and preachers of 'another Gospel' invaded the local churches. The problem still exists. Even during the true apostles' lifetime others claimed apostleship. The problem was not confined to Ephesus as Paul also wrote to Corinth about it. What Paul writes is well worth studying. We read three facts about those who create problems for true believers:

- How they operate.
- Who they serve.
- What their end will be.

Paul wrote, 'Suppose someone comes to you and preaches about a Jesus different from the Jesus we preached about. Or suppose you receive a message of good news different from the one you accepted earlier…People like that are false apostles. They work hard to trick others. They only pretend to be apostles of Christ. That comes as no surprise. Even Satan himself pretends to be an angel of light. So it doesn't surprise us that those who serve Satan pretend to be serving God. They will finally get exactly what they should.' 2 Corinthians 11:4 & 11:13-15. Who these false preachers are and what they preach will no doubt continually change but Jesus commends the Ephesians because they were not misled. They tested what they heard.

Question: As the Ephesian believers did not have the New Testament, what test could they have applied? Answer: Paul said these words to the Ephesians when he reviewed his visit to them. "'I was free of pride. I served the Lord with tears. I served him even though I was greatly tested by the evil plans of the Jews. You know I haven't let anyone keep me from preaching anything that would be helpful to you…'" Acts 20:19-20. Timothy and Tychicus also visited Ephesus to teach the believers and Paul also sent them a letter. So they received numerous warnings about false teachers and their teaching. We list the words that Jesus, John, and Paul used to describe these false teachers and their false message:

- 'Those who claim to be apostles but are not.'
- 'They are liars.'
- 'People like that are false apostles.'
- 'They work hard to trick others.'
- 'Those who serve Satan pretend to be serving God.'
- 'They will finally get exactly what they should.'
- 'Command people not to teach things that aren't true.'
- 'Don't let anyone fool you.'

Could these problems exist today? The above eight warnings should tell us that Satan will use all means to 'trick' believers of every generation into accepting lies and false teaching. Note that in 2 Corinthians the Gospel itself was under attack. Is the Gospel under attack today? Is 'today's Gospel' being:

- made more 'acceptable' to accommodate educated and respectable sinners living in 'Middle England?'
- made more 'chatty' because believers find it less embarrassing to mention sin and repentance privately?
- preached only to small groups made up of those who have shown an interest in spiritual things?

A Simple Test: In the next month count the times you hear:

- the words, 'sin' or 'repentance' in a sermon.
- the true Gospel, the one including sin and repentance.
- the false Gospel, the one omitting sin and repentance.

'You have been faithful…'

'"You have been faithful and have put up with a lot of trouble because of me. You have not given up."' Revelation 2:3. We have been considering what we have to do to be an overcomer. The short answer is that we have to overcome evil. How do we do that? Revelation 2:3 has three parts:

- 'You have been faithful.'
- 'You…have put up with a lot of trouble because of me.'
- 'You have not given up.'

'You have been faithful.' In Matthew 6:24 we read Jesus'

words, '"No one can serve two masters at the same time. He will hate one of them and love the other. Or he will be faithful to one and dislike the other. You can't serve God and Money at the same time."' The Ephesian believers made a decision to serve God. Prior to being saved they would have only been interested in the things of the world and chosen to be wealthy rather than faithful to God. When they were saved they turned their backs on the things of the world. Despite the problems that only those who are saved have, they remained faithful to God. Hence Jesus said to them, 'You…have put up with a lot of trouble because of me.'

If you are not yet saved, you will wonder why anyone would choose to have problems they could avoid by remaining unsaved. We must be totally frank and say that while some do not remain faithful, experience teaches that those who are saved never want to be 'unsaved.' Paul tells us why the Ephesian believers remained faithful despite their problems, 'At one time you were in the dark. But now you are in the light because of what the Lord has done.' Ephesians 5:8.

There are many references to 'light' and 'darkness' in the Bible illustrating contrasts such as that between Heaven and Hell. Jesus and Paul used the words to show the contrast between Salvation and sin and believers and unbelievers.

We cannot leave Ephesians 5:8 without a word to those who are not yet saved. We write in note form.

NOTES ON EPHESIANS 5:8.

'At one time you were in the dark. But now you are in the light because of what the Lord has done.'

The Ephesian believers' lives were divided into two periods. They were, without exception, born into the dark and they lived in the dark. Then a change occurred that will last for eternity. They began to live in the light.

- It was 'because of what the Lord had done' for them that this change occurred.
- If the Lord had not intervened on their behalf they

- ❖ would have lived in the dark all their lives.
- ❖ The Lord had intervened. They now lived in the light.
- ❖ They could not have done for themselves what the Lord had done for them.

Prior to being saved and living in the light, some were:

- ❖ Jews who worshipped God.
- ❖ Gentiles who worshipped idols.
- ❖ Judaism, the Jew's religion, could not have done for the Jews what the Lord had done for them.
- ❖ The idols worshipped by the Gentiles could not have done for them what the Lord had done for them.

Religious beliefs: Many contradict the Bible, e.g.

- ❖ 'We are all going to Heaven our own way.'
- ❖ 'We must do something to earn our Salvation.'
- ❖ 'God expects us to do the best we can.'

If Ephesians 5:8 has not persuaded you that only by what the Lord has done for you can you transfer from darkness to light, Ephesians 1:7, that 'sets the scene' for Ephesians 5:8, might assist. But first, you must realise that the New Testament describes Salvation in many ways:

- ❖ Paul wrote about darkness and light and how that because of what Jesus has done for each of us, we can decide to be saved and live in the light.
- ❖ Peter wrote about the slavery of sin and how that as Jesus' blood has paid the price to set us free from sin, we can decide to be saved from sin's slavery over us.

In Ephesians 1:7 Paul also writes how we can be free from the slavery of sin. Paul wrote, 'We have been set free because of what Christ has done. Through his blood our sins have been forgiven.' Consider Paul's words:

- ❖ 'what Christ has done'
- ❖ 'his blood,'
- ❖ 'our sins.

Spend time musing on these vital words. If you are still not persuaded questions might assist you to reflect on your personal need for Jesus to be your Saviour:

Question 1: Are you living in the dark?

Question 2: Are you a slave of sin?

Question 3: Have your sins been forgiven?

Question 4: Do you realise what Jesus has done for you?

Question 5: Have you ever personally thanked Jesus for taking all your punishment and shedding His Own blood so that God could forgive your sin and Heaven could be you eternal home? If you have not, do not read on until you are sure that the Salvation experience that Paul wrote about in the two verses quoted below is your personal experience too.

'We have been set free because of what Christ has done. Through his blood our sins have been forgiven.' Ephesians 1:7.

'At one time you were in the dark. But now you are in the light because of what the Lord has done.' Ephesians 5:8.

The Book of Life Belongs to the Lamb

We know from the New Testament that 'the Lamb' refers to Jesus. He was sacrificed and He shed His blood for the sin of the world. The numerous Old Testament sacrifices of perfect lambs over many centuries pointed to the day when God 'placed on Jesus the sins of all of us' and Jesus:

- 'suffered the things we should have suffered.'
- 'took on himself the pain that should have been ours.'
- 'was pierced because we had sinned.'
- was 'crushed because we had done what was evil.'
- was 'punished to make us whole again.'

Only innocent and perfect lambs could be a picture of Jesus, the sinless Saviour. Only perfect lambs could be sacrificed.

Isaiah: The quotations above are from Isaiah 53. Verses 6-7 need careful consideration. 'All of us are like sheep. We have wandered away from God. All of us have turned to our own way. And the LORD has placed on his servant the sins of all of us. He was beaten down and made to suffer. But he didn't open his mouth. He was led away like a sheep to be killed. Lambs are silent while their wool is being cut off. In the same way, he didn't open his mouth.' Isaiah 53:6-7. We have quoted many verses from Isaiah already but Isaiah has sixty-six chapters and there are in excess of twenty references to him in the New Testament. Jesus and the New Testament writers always compliment Him. For instance:

- Jesus: Matthew 15:7. Jesus said to some Pharisees and teachers of the law. 'You hypocrites! Isaiah was right when he prophesied…'
- Paul: Acts 28:25. 'The Holy Spirit spoke the truth to your ancestors when he said through Isaiah the prophet…'

No one would need persuading that Isaiah was a good man who was greatly used by God. But no matter how good he was, he, like us, was a sinner. But unlike so many of us, he was willing to admit he was a sinner. He wrote:

- 'All of us are like sheep.'
- 'We have wandered away from God.'
- 'All of us have turned to our own way.'
- 'The LORD has placed on his servant the sins of all of us.'

Note the small vital words, 'us,' 'we,' 'our,' and 'own.' Isaiah associated himself with the sinful people that God had sent him to preach to. Isaiah brings two facts to our attention:

- His sins and our sins were placed on Jesus.
- He was saved on the same basis that we can be saved.

If you want to be saved, like Isaiah you will have to admit that you are a sinner and that Jesus died for your sins.

The Silent Lamb

Sheep do not resist and are silent when taken for slaughter and lambs are silent while their wool is shorn so Isaiah gives us 'a picture' of Jesus who silently suffered for our sin.

A Great Misunderstanding

Teaching the Bible to youngsters gives them a good start in life. But one problem is hard to avoid. They can be given the impression that Jesus has only the attributes of love and gentleness. And it is not just Bible stories that can mislead them. Hymns such as 'Gentle Jesus meek and mild...' can reinforce the view that God will not judge sinners. But even a cursory reading of the Bible shows that God hates and punishes sin. Jesus mentioned Hell as being a real place of punishment that needs to be avoided. Exceptionally, the Bible mentions God's immediate punishment for sin. We read what actually happened to those who sinned. It does not make for pleasant reading. Those who teach children either avoid referring to it or if they have to, they minimise its severity. Hence it is not surprising that when in later years some read about God's Judgment in Revelation or other passages in The Gospels for the first time they are shocked. Experience teaches that even those who have never challenged what they have read in the Bible find it hard to accept the severity of God's Judgment for sin.

Many attending non-Bible based churches have been misled over many years into believing a variety of notions such as:

- They will go to Heaven as everyone is going to Heaven.
- Our future in Heaven or Hell will be decided after death and God's decision will take our good deeds into account.

Many do not read the Bible for themselves and consequently they have held these and similar views for many years. It comes as quite a shock when they realise that:

- They decide their own eternal future before they die.
- If they do not accept Jesus as their Saviour they:
    - Reject the only way to Heaven.
    - Will one day face Jesus as their Judge.

The Bible's Critics

Many are put off reading the Bible because they hear this and that about it and it is not fashionable to show an interest in it. But experience teaches that those who criticise the Bible have little knowledge of it. This is the incredible reality:

- Those who never read the Bible criticise it even though:
    - They do not criticise other books they have not read.
    - They do not criticise films or plays they have not seen.
- Those who read the Bible do not criticise it.

Many do not realise that their vehemently prejudiced attitude to the Bible betrays their hope that the Bible is not authentic.

Do not be reluctant to read the Bible. God speaks to us as we read His Word. That cannot be said of any other book. Humbly ask God to guide you to the truth He wants you to know. You might have to swim against the tide of popular opinion. You might be ridiculed. But Jesus promised that those who seek will find. As you would expect, experience teaches that Jesus has always been as good as His word.

God's Judgment

Those who denigrate the Bible and openly oppose God and Christianity are not slow to point out those occasions where God's Judgment appears at first sight to be arbitrary, unfair and contrary to the view that God is a God of love. Some of God's Judgments involve the death of children and the Bible's opponents relish referring to them as 'innocent children.' But the very fact that we can read about incidents that on the surface give an unfavourable view of God proves that the Bible has not been 'doctored' to make it more acceptable. The Bible's opponents overlook this. It adds substantial evidential weight to the Bible's authenticity.

But we must not overlook the fact that it is impossible for those who are sinful and who live in a sinful world to fully understand the ways of a holy and righteous God. This situation does not change when sinners are saved. It is not possible for believers to know 'all of God's ways' because the Bible does not have 'all the answers' and there is no other divine source of knowledge.

The Holy Spirit and Unbelievers

In John 16:8, (GNB) Jesus said that when the Holy Spirit came He would '...prove to the people of the world that they are wrong about sin and about what is right and about God's judgment.' So Jesus stated that the people of the world were wrong about three spiritual matters:

- 'Sin.'
- 'What is right.'
- 'God's judgment.'

It is the work of the Holy Spirit, and not the work of believers, to prove divine truth 'to the people of the world.' Unsurprisingly, no exceptions are mentioned. If unbelievers will not accept what the Holy Spirit says, they will not be persuaded by believer's arguments however eloquently put.

Believers live in the light but the Bible states that there are things that 'no human mind has conceived' that 'God has prepared for those who love him.' So believers will only find out more about what God has done, is doing, and will do when they arrive in Heaven. In the meantime they are willing to take God at His word and unquestionably trust Him:

- Trusting God divides believers from unbelievers.
- Demands for proof divides unbelievers from believers.

God Has Proved His Love

This is the reason why believers do not:

- Challenge God.
- Seek to justify God's Judgment to unbelievers.

We could quote many verses to support the truth that God has proved His love but the constraints of space limit us to these two. 'How did God show his love for us? He sent his one and only Son into the world. He sent him so we could receive life through him. What is love? It is not that we loved God. It is that he loved us and sent his Son to give his life to pay for our sins.' 1 John 4:9-10. John 'hits the nail on the head' in these two verses:

- God loved us when we were in our sin and unlovable.
- God loved us when we did not love Him.
- God loved us enough to send His Son to die for our sins.

Here is an amazing truth! God loves those who do not love

Him and who either deny His existence or criticise Him for the way He judges. They are not immediately punished for their sins because God loves them. We read, 'The LORD loves us very much. So we haven't been completely destroyed. His loving concern never fails.' Lamentations 3:22. Those who do not love God are not destroyed. They have the opportunity to repent and be forgiven. If they accept Jesus as their Saviour and Lord they can have all the blessings that God has for those who respond to His love.

Argument and Persuasion

We state categorically that argument and persuasion will not convert an unbeliever to a believer. We repeat our previous comments on John 16:8. Jesus said that when the Holy Spirit came He would '...prove to the people of the world that they are wrong about sin and about what is right and about God's judgment.' It is the work of the Holy Spirit and not the work of believers to prove divine truth 'to the people of the world.'

In 1 Thessalonians we read a verse about the Holy Spirit that is well worth memorising. Paul was second to none in the skills of argument and persuasion but he wrote, '...our gospel came to you not simply with words but also with power, with the Holy Spirit and deep conviction. You know how we lived among you for your sake.' 1 Thessalonians 1:5. Take time to study this verse and as you do, compare present-day evangelical views to Paul's view. He mentions:

- 'Our Gospel.'
- 'Words.'
- 'Power.'
- 'The Holy Spirit.'
- 'Deep conviction.'
- 'How we lived.'

'Our Gospel' - Those who for any reason want to change 'the Gospel' should first ask themselves whether they are permitted to do so. The obvious question is this. Who does the Gospel belong to? The Thessalonians could never claim that the Gospel was conceived and owned by them as Paul wrote, 'our Gospel came to you.' So those who want to 'sidestep' the truth that all have sinned or 'soft-pedal' the need for repentance should not only question their motives but their authority to change the Gospel.

'Words' - Whatever words are used, the Gospel must be preached. We have already read what it must contain to be the 'true' Gospel. So if you desire to preach the 'true' Gospel, you cannot please yourself what you preach because additions or omissions turn the 'true' Gospel into a false gospel. If you do not preach the 'true' Gospel you will have missed an opportunity for unbelievers to be saved. Those who need God's Salvation need to hear the 'true' Gospel.

'Power' - 'Power' means 'miraculous power.' We witness a miracle occurs each time a person is saved. Read how this divine transaction is referred to in the New Testament and treasure the miracle of God's Salvation. Unbelievers are:

- 'transferred from darkness to light.'
- 'transferred from the power of Satan unto God, that they may receive forgiveness of sins...'
- 'saved from the kingdom of darkness and brought into the kingdom of the Son God loves.'

Have you experienced the miracle of God's Salvation in your own life? Because of 'what the Lord has done' for you, you could do so right now. Why remain unsaved and in the darkness when you could be "transferred from the power of Satan unto God?'

'The Holy Spirit' - Salvation is a divine transaction involving God and a sinner. Many think that there must be some human involvement. The Bible and experience teach that God speaks to sinners through the Bible. There is no doubt that those who read the Bible seeking Salvation discover for themselves that Jesus can save them. Believers can have the privilege of preaching the Gospel that directs sinners to the Saviour. But if believers do not preach the true Gospel, no one will be saved.

Believers are both instructed and privileged to take the Gospel to the world but they must not think that their personal involvement is essential. Church history is cluttered with the names of those who have underestimated the power of the Holy Spirit and overestimated their own importance. A believer is privileged to preach the Gospel but thereafter, it is the work of the Holy Spirit to introduce sinners to Jesus.

'Deep conviction' - These words and their context have been variously translated. We quote from three translations:

GNB: '…we brought the Good News to you, not with words only, but also with power and the Holy Spirit, and with complete conviction of its truth.' 1 Thessalonians 1:5.

NIV: '…our gospel came to you not simply with words but also with power, with the Holy Spirit and deep conviction.'

GW: 'the Good News we brought came to you not only with words but also with power, with the Holy Spirit, and with complete certainty.' 1 Thessalonians 1:5.

Those who attend court know how difficult it is to challenge witnesses who testify from personal experience. People can change their opinions. No one can change an experience. Paul, and those who assisted him to preach the Gospel, had themselves believed it. They knew from their own experience that it had changed their lives. So when they preached to others, they had no doubts at all that what the Gospel had done for them, it could do for those who believed it. No wonder Paul wrote that he preached the Gospel with:

GNB. 'complete conviction of its truth.'

NIV. 'deep conviction.'

GW. 'complete certainty.'

IMPORTANT: The truths above that relate to the Gospel itself and the truths that follow about a believer's behaviour must not be separated. They are undeniably linked.

- ❖ The Gospel changes lives and the Holy Spirit produces holiness in believers.
- ❖ If there is no change in the behaviour of a person who claims to be saved, you would be naive to believe them.

'How we lived' - 'You know how we lived among you' follows the words, 'not simply with words.' Paul's and his companions' conduct is linked to the Gospel they preached: Paul was saved. The change in Paul's life was visible, hence he could write to the Thessalonians, 'you know how we lived among you.' Paul had nothing to be ashamed of. On the contrary, he considered that his life showed that the Gospel was authentic. So he could add that what he did, not only what he said, had benefited the Thessalonians.

Some try to justify their refusal to be saved by saying that they are as good as those who are saved. When we put what Jesus did on the Cross so that they might be saved alongside this excuse and any and every other excuse, we see excuses for what they really are:

- A refusal to repent and believe the Gospel.
- A rejection of Jesus as Saviour and Lord.

But we must be totally frank and state that unbelievers do not expect believers to misbehave. Who is going to listen to what a misbehaving believer has to say about sin, judgment and the inherent power of the Gospel to change the lives of those who believe it?

Heaven's Books

The Lamb's Book of Life is not the only 'book' that John saw in his vision. When John wrote Revelation there were no books as such. Printing was unknown. Scrolls made of the papyrus bark from Egypt were common. Some translators of the Bible into English use 'scroll,' where others use 'book.' Although the extract from Revelation 5 below from the NIrV uses 'scroll,' we will use both words in our commentary.

Some scrolls were 'private and confidential.' Such scrolls had a seal on them and if it was broken, you would know that 'for your eyes only' information could have been read by others. John sobbed loud and for a long time when he thought that there was a problem over one particular scroll that had seven seals. He thought that there was no one worthy enough to break the seals and to read the scroll.

A Scroll With Seven Seals: Revelation 5

Read the following extract from Revelation 5 and do not read on until you know what will happen in Heaven in a coming day. 'I saw a scroll in the right hand of the One sitting on the throne. The scroll had writing on both sides. It was sealed with seven seals. I saw a mighty angel calling out in a loud voice, “Who is worthy to break the seals and open the scroll?” But no one in heaven or on earth or under the earth could open the scroll. No one could even look inside it. I cried and cried because no one was found who was worthy to open the scroll or look inside. Then one of the elders said to me, “Do not cry! The Lion of the tribe of Judah has won the battle. He is the Root of David. He is able to break the seven seals and open the scroll.” Then I saw a Lamb that looked as if he had been put to death. He stood in the center of the area around the throne. The Lamb was surrounded by the four living creatures and the elders...The Lamb came and took the scroll from the right hand of the One sitting on the throne. Then the four living creatures and the 24 elders fell down in front of the Lamb. Each one had a harp. They were holding golden bowls full of incense, which stand for the prayers of God's people...Here is the new song they sang. “You are worthy to take the scroll and break open its seals. You are worthy because you were put to death. With your blood you bought people for God. They come from every tribe, language, people and nation...Then I looked and heard the voice of millions and millions of angels. They surrounded the throne. They surrounded the living creatures and the elders. In a loud voice they sang, “The Lamb, who was put to death, is worthy! He is worthy to receive power and wealth and wisdom and strength! He is worthy to receive honor and glory and praise!” All creatures in heaven, on earth, under the earth, and on the sea, and all that is in them, were singing. I heard them say, “May praise and honor for ever and ever be given to the One who sits on the throne and to the Lamb! Give them glory and power for ever and ever!” The four living creatures said, “Amen.” And the elders fell down and worshiped.’ Extract from Revelation 5.

Revelation 5

The One who sits on the throne is God. John saw millions of angels. He records that one angel shouted out, “Who is worthy to break the seals and open the scroll?” The response caused John’s sorrow. Read his words and the places mentioned. It seems that a search was made everywhere but he concluded that no one anywhere was worthy to open the scroll. He was only quiet when given information about the worthy One. John knew what the Old Testament taught about the Messiah. He had also heard Jesus teach Old Testament truths about Himself. He could have identified the worthy One from the descriptions, 'The Lion of the tribe of Judah has won the battle' and 'He is the Root of David.'

- The lion was a creature of majesty and strength.
- Judah was the leading tribe of the Kingdom of Judah. King David and the royal line belonged to it. The Jews believed that the Messiah would come from this tribe based on God's promise to King David of an everlasting throne for his offspring. In the New Testament Jesus is described as a member of the tribe of Judah by lineage.

'He is the Root of David.' God promised King David that the Christ, 'the Messiah,' would come from his offspring. But the One who was worthy was described as 'the Root of David.' He must therefore have existed before David.

John may have known that the worthy Person was Jesus. He was with Jesus when the chief priests, the teachers of the law and the elders came to challenge Him.

Revelation 5 and Luke 20:41-47

Jesus' words in Luke 20 tie in with Revelation 5. '"Why do people say that the Christ is the Son of David? David himself says in the Book of Psalms, "'The Lord said to my Lord, "Sit at my right hand until I put your enemies under your control."' David calls him 'Lord.' So how can he be David's son?" 'All the people were listening. Jesus said to his disciples, "Watch out for the teachers of the law. They like to walk around in long robes. They love to be greeted in the market places. They love to have the most important seats in the synagogues. They also love to have the places of honor at dinners. They take over the houses of widows. They say long prayers to show off. God will punish those men very much."'

A Note of Caution: Jesus and the Religious Leaders.

A substantial number of verses, forty-seven in total, are devoted to just one of the confrontations that Jesus had with religious people. We deal with Jesus' warnings about religious leaders and teachers first. We cannot comment on

Luke 20 without first mentioning verses 45-47. We have previously warned of the danger of religion as it is possible to be religious and not be saved. Many do not realise that good works and religious observances do not count with a holy God who hates sin. Verses 45-47 refer to God's punishment for hypocrites. The religious people:

- walk round in long robes.
- like to be noticed, have the most important seats in the church and the places of honour at dinners.

It was not just the religious leaders' spirituality that Jesus challenged. He challenged their scriptural knowledge. Jesus' words may shock some who have assumed that those who wear 'religious clothing' must be spiritual and knowledgeable.

- Luke 20 proves that on a number of important matters the religious teachers were wrong. Their congregations would doubtless think that their teachers ought to know what the Old Testament actually taught.
- Those who are familiar with The Gospels will know of other occasions when Jesus corrected the Jewish leaders' and teacher's doctrinal errors.

Regrettably, little has changed in two thousand years. Many do not read the Bible for themselves and accept what they hear from the pulpit assuming it to be biblically correct.

"Why do people say…?" Jesus asked this question because:

- What the spiritual leaders taught was not the whole truth.
- The spiritual leaders could have found out the whole truth from the Old Testament.
- The verse quoted by Jesus from Psalm 110:1 was either being ignored or misinterpreted by the spiritual leaders.
  - They were not new or recent words. They were written centuries before by King David.
  - Generation after generation had been misled by these so-called spiritual men.

These verses should be a warning to everyone who claims that their church and its teaching dates back centuries but never concern themselves to read the Bible for themselves.

Question 1: Do you accept what your church has been teaching for centuries, or do you read the Bible for yourself?

Question 2: Do you preach what your church has been preaching for centuries or do you read the Bible for yourself?

Jesus: The Christ and David's Lord.

- John heard Jesus say the words we read in Luke 20 above. The Christ was David's Lord.
- In Revelation 5 Jesus, seen by John as 'a Lamb,' is 'the Lion of the tribe of Judah,' 'the Root of David.'
- King David's tribe was Judah. David headed the Jewish royal family.

John saw a Lamb. He majestically headed His own tribe of Judah. He was the Root of the Jewish royal family. Hence, the Lamb was Jesus, and He was David's Lord.

Jesus: The Lamb.

Seeing a Lamb when he was looking for a Lion was not John's only surprise. The Lamb showed the marks of death but it was alive and standing. The Lamb was the centre of Heaven's attention. How many only think of Jesus' death and ignore His triumphant resurrection and ascension?

The Lamb: 'The Lion of the Tribe of Judah.'

What 'battle' had 'the Lion' won? The elder did not say but when John looked for a Lion, he saw a Lamb. What he tells us about the Lamb enables us to state with certainty that:

- 'The battle' was fought two thousand years ago.
- Jesus defeated Satan, 'the Devil.' By dying and being raised from death Jesus achieved an immediate and eternal victory over Satan's rule, authority and power.

Jesus' victory had an immediate and a postponed result. When Jesus died and rose again Satan was defeated but not eliminated. The immediate results of Jesus' victory are that:

- Those who believe the Gospel are immediately released from Satan's power.
- Believers need not fear death. Satan still rules over death but believers, like Jesus, will be brought back to life.

At a future time:

- ❖ Jesus will destroy all evil rule, authority and power.
- ❖ All Jesus' enemies will be under His control.
- ❖ Jesus will finally destroy death, His last enemy.

Reading the following verses that explain why Jesus' death and resurrection guarantee that 'those who belong to Him' need not fear death. 'But Christ really has been raised from the dead. He is the first of all those who will rise…But here is the order of events. Christ is the first of those who rise from the dead. When he comes back, those who belong to him will be raised. Then the end will come. Christ will destroy all rule, authority and power…Christ must rule until he has put all his enemies under his control. The last enemy that will be destroyed is death. Extract from 1 Corinthians 15:20-26. 'Those children have bodies made out of flesh and blood. So Jesus became human like them in order to die for them. By doing that, he could destroy the one who rules over the kingdom of death. I'm talking about the devil. Jesus could set people free who were afraid of death. All their lives they were held as slaves by that fear.' Hebrews 2:14-15.

We humans will never know the extent of the evil forces at work in this world. The Bible mentions their existence but little information is given. But what we know with certainty is that Jesus' death and resurrection defeated everything that is evil. Satan's personal punishment is stated in Revelation 20: 'Then the Devil, who deceived them, was thrown into the lake of fire and sulphur… tormented day and night forever and ever.' Revelation 20:10. Until that time comes, Satan actively promotes and encourages evil and he seeks to prevent unbelievers being saved. Hence Paul calls him, 'The god of this world' in the verses we shall consider next in 2 Corinthians 4.

Satan and the Gospel: 2 Corinthians 4.

Paul was working with Timothy when he wrote these words that reinforce the truths we have considered. 'So because of God's mercy, we have work to do. He has given it to us. And we don't give up. Instead, we have given up doing secret and shameful things. We don't twist God's word. In fact, we do just the opposite. We present the truth plainly. In the sight of God, we make our appeal to everyone's sense of what is right and wrong. Suppose our good news is covered with a veil. Then it is veiled to those who are dying. The god of this world has blinded the minds of those who don't believe. They can't see the light of the good news of Christ's glory. He is the likeness of God. We do not preach about ourselves. We preach about Jesus Christ. We say that he is Lord. And we serve you because of him. God said, "Let light shine out of darkness." He made his light shine in our hearts. It shows us the light of God's glory in the face of Christ. Treasure is kept in clay jars. In the same way, we have the treasure of the good news in these earthly bodies of ours. That shows that the mighty power of the good news comes from God. It doesn't come from us.' 2 Corinthians 4:1-7. Paul states that:

- 'God is merciful': This is good news for sinners because forgiveness is available to those who believe in Jesus.
- They were doing God's work: No matter how long we are engaged in Gospel work, it never becomes 'our work.'
- 'We do not give up' God's work: Quitting for any reason is not an option. Retirement is not mentioned either. Servants only stop when told to do so by their master.

Note the contrast in 2 Corinthians 4:1-2 that emphasises the distinction between believers and unbelievers:

- Verse 1: 'We don't give up' God's work.
- Verse 2: 'We have given up secret and shameful things.'

Paul and Timothy had devout religious backgrounds. But, like every sinner who has been saved, Paul's and Timothy's lifestyles changed. Before they were saved they did 'secret and shameful things.' After they were saved Paul could write:

- 'We have given up doing secret and shameful things.'
- 'We don't twist God's word. In fact, we do just the opposite. We present the truth plainly.' Then as now, some preachers could not honestly write Paul's words.

If what we preach is 'God's word,' why do some think that they have the right to alter it to suit particular congregations or to save offending some social class?

As you read the remaining verses in 2 Corinthians 4, you can tell from Paul's words that Satan is very successful in his work of keeping unbelievers blinded to 'the good news of Christ's glory.' Paul gives Satan the title of, 'The god of this world.' You cannot be surprised at his title. Paul wrote two thousand years ago. Satan still works to prevent the majority from being saved.

- Have you ever realised that only the Gospel can free you from Satan's power over you?
- Paul wrote, 'That shows that the mighty power of the good news comes from God. It doesn't come from us.'
- If only congregations realised that the Gospel itself is 'the mighty power' that saves, they might:
    - stop wanting to hear preachers who entertain them.
    - start wanting to hear preachers who 'preach about Jesus Christ' and 'say that he is Lord.'

What Paul wrote to Timothy will shock those unaware of it: '...the time will come when people will not put up with sound doctrine. Instead, to suit their own desires, they will gather around them a great number of teachers to say what their itching ears want to hear. They will turn their ears away from the truth and turn aside to myths.' 2 Timothy 4:3-4.

Christ's Glory and 'the god of this world.'

When we considered the Old Testament and the Gospel we noted that the Gospel consisted of 'the sufferings and Christ and the glory that would follow.' Hence, as Paul refers to the Gospel, he says of unbelievers, 'They can't see the light of the good news of Christ's glory' because 'the god of this world has blinded the minds of those who don't believe.' 2 Corinthians 4:4. Satan's work of 'blinding the minds of those who don't believe' has been successful. How many today, even churchgoers,

- are unaware of 'the good news of Christ's glory?'
- live without acknowledging that 'Jesus is Lord,' and more importantly, Jesus is their Lord?

Even though the Gospel is 'the good news of Christ's glory,' how many today have no personal experience of worshipping

Jesus as their Lord and Saviour?' We write later about a day when all who have not admitted that 'Jesus is Lord' in their lifetimes will have no option but to do so.

Satan's Rule, Authority and Power

When Jesus told Paul he would preach the Gospel, Jesus said, '...I am sending you to them to open their eyes. I want you to turn them from darkness to light. I want you to turn them from Satan's power to God. I want their sins to be forgiven. They will be forgiven when they believe in me...' Acts 26:17-18.

Paul's three tasks as a Gospel preacher were to:

- 'Open their eyes.'
- 'Turn them from darkness to light.'
- 'Turn them from Satan's power to God.'

'Open their eyes'

Satan wants to keep unbelievers:

- From seeing the light of Christ's glory.
- Blinded to the truth.

The Gospel can open blind eyes.

'Turn them from darkness to light'

Satan wants to keep unbelievers:

- Living in the darkness of sin.
- Unforgiven.

Jesus said, 'I want their sins to be forgiven. They will be forgiven when they believe in me...' Do not let Satan keep you in the dark with your sins unforgiven. Jesus' victory over Satan can be your victory over Satan too.

'Turn them from Satan's power to God'

- Satan has unbelievers in his power.
- Satan rules over all that is evil. Many seem willing to submit to his authority over them.

The Gospel is that Jesus died for your sins so that He could forgive you and be your Saviour and Lord. We repeat that Jesus' victory over Satan can free you from Satan's power over you but only if you repent and believe in Jesus. Do you want Him to be your Saviour and Lord? Are you willing to repent and bow your knee to Him? The alternative is to live in Satan's grasp.

Revelation 5: Only The Lamb was Worthy

John tells us that after a search was made everywhere, only the Lamb was worthy. He took the scroll from God. That was when the singing of three separate songs, by three separate groups began. There are important differences in the words of these three songs but before considering them, we must mention that only Jesus is entitled to our worship. He does not share that right with anyone. Many throughout the world worship Jesus' mother Mary. Consider what we read in Matthew 2:11, often associated with the 'Christmas Story.' 'The Wise Men went to the house. There they saw the child with his mother Mary. They bowed down and worshiped him. Then they opened their treasures. They gave him gold, incense and myrrh.' The wise men's worship and gifts were only for Jesus. Why? Jesus was, is, and always will be divine. The wise men's gifts indicated that Jesus came into the world to die. Matthew 2 totally agrees with what John tells us in Revelation 5. Both in the text and in the songs only a living Lamb who once died is said to be worthy. So we repeat that only Jesus is worthy.

Jesus Is Worthy Of and Entitled To Our Worship

Consider the songs that John heard. The living creatures, the elders and the angels state why they only worship Jesus. He is unique. He and He alone died to save sinful man. That is why, when Peter preached he said about Jesus, '"You can't be saved by believing in anyone else. God has given us no other name under heaven that will save us."' Acts 4:12.

Translators of the Bible into English seem to agree that the living creatures and elders sang their worship to Jesus but disagree as to whether the angels' and the created beings' words were sung or spoken. But it is their words' that really matter. As the NIrV that we quote from refers to 'songs,' we do the same and refer to 'songs,' 'singers' and 'singing.'

The First Song: Revelation 9-10. The Living Creatures and Elders. 'You are worthy to take the scroll and break open its seals. You are worthy because you were put to death. With your blood you bought people for God. They come from every tribe, language, people and nation. You have made them members of a royal family. You have made them priests to serve our God. They will rule on the earth.'

The Second Song: Revelation 5:12. The Angels, Living Creatures and Elders 'The Lamb, who was put to death, is worthy! He is worthy to receive power and wealth and wisdom and strength! He is worthy to receive honor and glory and praise!'

The Third Song: Revelation 5:13. All Created Beings. 'May praise and honor for ever and ever be given to the One who sits on the throne and to the Lamb! Give them glory and power for ever...'

The Living Creatures, Elders, Angels and Created Beings

We cannot go into detail about the allegory or picture language used by John but he clearly identifies three different groups of singers. The name of each group, where they are and what they sing tell us that they each have a different relationship to Jesus. That is why three separate songs are required. We can best illustrate this by commenting on the angels first.

Angels: Angels who sin cannot be saved. We read in Peter and Jude. 'God did not spare angels when they sinned. Instead, he sent them to hell...He will keep them there until he judges them.' 2 Peter 2:4. 'Some of the angels didn't stay where they belonged...They are held by chains that last forever...' Jude 1:6. The millions of angels who have not sinned are in Heaven and they, together with the living creatures and elders, sing, 'The Lamb, who was put to death, is worthy! He is worthy to receive power and wealth and wisdom and strength! He is worthy to receive honor and glory and praise!' Revelation 5:12.

The angels in Heaven must have been shocked when they looked down and saw the appalling treatment suffered by

Jesus as cruel men crucified Him. They witnessed the Lamb being put to death and they refer to it in their worship.

The Living Creatures and Elders

The word 'living' is exclusive to this group:

- ❖ They are 'born again' and have eternal life.

They are 'creatures.' In that respect they are the same as all other creatures but the difference that really counts is:

- ❖ The majority of creatures refused to be saved.
- ❖ Only a minority of creatures:
  - ❖ Repented.
  - ❖ Accepted Jesus as their Saviour and Lord.
  - ❖ Had their names written in the Lamb's Book of Life.

That is why the 'living creatures sing about:

- ❖ Jesus' death and Jesus' blood:
  - ❖ Jesus took God's punishment for sin and He died so that sinners could be not only be forgiven, but be as sinless as Jesus and enter Heaven.
  - ❖ Jesus shed His own precious blood so that sinners could be redeemed from Satan's slave market of sin and 'bought for God.'

Note their words carefully: "With your blood you bought people for God." As we can read, not everyone has been 'bought for God.' Many chose to remain in the slave market as Satan's slaves. You know your own spiritual condition. Can you make the above words personal to yourself and say to Jesus right now with total certainty, "With your blood you bought me for God?" If you can, one day you will be one of those you have read about in Revelation 5 who worship Jesus. We do not know how many will have accepted Jesus as Saviour and Lord by the time this event occurs but we do know that you can choose to be one of them as you read these words.

The Created Beings

Not all the created beings are in Heaven. Some are, '...on earth, under the earth, and on the sea...' Revelation 5:13.

But note that we also read in Revelation 5:13 that 'all…were singing' Why are these otherwise simple words so weighty? Consider where the singers are and what happens next.

The Singers in Heaven

They willingly worship Jesus. They are looking forward to a blissful eternity in His presence.

The Singers Not in Heaven: The Unsaved.

All the unsaved will sing, but they are not in Heaven. The Lake of Fire for eternity awaits them. Despite knowing their punishment, they will have no choice but to praise Jesus. God will not force the unsaved to praise Jesus now. They can proudly boast that they would prefer Hell to Heaven because all their friends are there and laugh at similar comments. They can make light of sin and Jesus' death but all you will hear from them as they await to be thrown into the Lake of Fire is, "May praise and honor for ever and ever be given to the One who sits on the throne and to the Lamb! Give them glory and power for ever…' Revelation 5:13.

A Second Chance for the Unsaved?

Some think that this occasion will provide 'a second chance' to be saved for those who die unsaved. When we have considered the different songs that the three groups sing you will realise why there is no 'second chance.'

The Three Songs

The first group sing their song and then join in the second group's song. Both groups then join in the third group's song but note the all-important differences between the words of the three songs. The words reflect the fact that each group has a different relationship to Jesus.

What a Difference Being Saved Makes!

- Some are saved: the living creatures and the elders.
- Some cannot be saved: the angels.
- Some are unsaved: the created beings not in Heaven.

Let us prove this to you in question and multiple-choice form.

Question 1: Which group do not refer to Jesus' death? Is it:

a. The living creatures and the elders?

b. The angels?

c. The created beings that are not in Heaven?

The answer is c. This should not surprise. When they had the opportunity to be saved, they ignored Jesus' death on their behalf. This is reflected in their song. They only give praise, honour and glory to God and to Jesus.

Question 2: Which group refer to the death of Jesus but not Jesus' blood which bought people for God? Is it:

a. The living creatures and the elders?

b. The angels?

c. The created beings that are not in Heaven?

The answer is b. This should cause no surprise either. Jesus did not shed His blood for the angels who sinned but, in contrast to the unsaved, the angels did not ignore what Jesus did when He came to Earth to die for our sins. Consider what the New Testament tells us about the angels.

Jesus and the Angels

The angels announced Jesus' birth and cared for Him after He was tempted by Satan. They were active before Jesus' death and after His resurrection. Prior to His arrest He prayed to His Father. Jesus was sinless and He knew that His time to be crucified for our sins had come.

These words from Paul explain what Jesus did when He was crucified and died for our sins. 'Christ didn't have any sin. But God made him become sin for us. So we can be made right with God because of what Christ has done for us.' 2 Corinthians 5:21. Keep Paul's words in mind as we read Jesus' prayer. '...he got down on his knees and prayed. He said, "Father, if you are willing, take this cup of suffering away from me. But do what you want, not what I want." An angel from heaven appeared to Jesus and gave him strength. Because he was very sad and troubled, he prayed even harder. His sweat was like drops of blood falling to the ground.' Luke 22:41-44.

Never minimise what:

- Jesus was willing to do for sinful man.
- Jesus endured as 'God made him become sin for us.'

Prior to the crucifixion a large crowd came to arrest Jesus. Peter wanted to protect Him but Jesus said to him, '"Do you think I can't ask my Father for help? He would send an army of more than 70,000 angels right away."' Mathew 26:53. Peter did not then grasp that Jesus loved us so much that He was willing to die for us.

An angel is mentioned after Jesus' resurrection. Once again we read of the religious hierarchy's wickedness. Even when proved wrong, they bribed, lied and deceived. 'The Sabbath day was now over. It was dawn on the first day of the week. Mary Magdalene and the other Mary went to look at the tomb. There was a powerful earthquake. An angel of the Lord came down from heaven. The angel went to the tomb. He rolled back the stone and sat on it. His body shone like lightning. His clothes were as white as snow. The guards were so afraid of him that they shook and became like dead men. The angel said to the women, "Don't be afraid. I know that you are looking for Jesus, who was crucified. He is not here! He has risen, just as he said he would! Come and see the place where he was lying. Go quickly! Tell his disciples, 'He has risen from the dead. He is going ahead of you into Galilee. There you will see him.' Now I have told you." So the women hurried away from the tomb. They were afraid, but they were filled with joy. They ran to tell the disciples. Suddenly Jesus met them. "Greetings!" he said. They came to him, took hold of his feet and worshiped him. Then Jesus said to them, "Don't be afraid. Go and tell my brothers to go to Galilee. There they will see me." While the women were on their way, some of the guards went into the city. They reported to the chief priests all that had happened. When the chief priests met with the elders, they came up with a plan. They gave the soldiers a large amount of money. They told the soldiers, "We want you to say, 'His disciples came during the night. They stole his body while we were sleeping.' If the governor hears this report, we will pay him off. That will keep you out of trouble." So the soldiers took the money and did as they were told. This story has spread all around among the Jews to this very day.' Matthew 28:1-15. Prior to Jesus' ascension, He told His disciples that they would receive the Holy Spirit's power to be witnesses of His resurrection. The Holy Spirit's personal participation in the Gospel must not be minimised. Note the involvement of two angels in the following verses. They are referred to as 'men' which is consistent with what the Bible teaches about how they look. Only cherubim and seraphs have wings. Halos and similar things, like much that you will find in Christendom, but not in the Bible, are figments of man's vivid imagination. Jesus said, '"But you will receive power when the Holy Spirit comes on you. Then you will be my witnesses in Jerusalem. You will be my witnesses in all Judea and Samaria. And you will be my witnesses from one end of the earth to the other." After Jesus said this, he was taken up to heaven. They watched until a cloud hid him from their sight. While he was going up, they kept on looking at the sky. Suddenly two men dressed in white clothing stood beside them. "Men of Galilee," they said, "why do you stand here looking at the sky? Jesus has been taken away from you into heaven. But he will come back in the same way you saw him go."' Acts 1:8-11.

We wrote about the angels after we asked the question, 'Which group refer to the death of Jesus but not Jesus' blood which bought people for God? The answer was the angels. We wanted to show their involvement in Jesus' birth, life, death, resurrection and ascension to support our statement that, 'in contrast to the unsaved, the angels did not ignore what Jesus did when He came to Earth to die for our sins.

The 'Second Chance' Theory

Contrary to the clear teaching of the Bible, there are those who think that when the unsaved praise Jesus, they will have a 'second chance' to be saved. But those who are saved and the angels are singing in Heaven to Jesus who is also in Heaven. The unsaved are not in Heaven. Their names are not in the Lamb's Book of Life. They will praise Jesus before they are thrown into the Lake of Fire. They will sing, 'May praise and honor for ever and ever be given to the One who sits on the throne and to the Lamb! Give them glory and power for ever…' Revelation 5:13.

The word ‘worship’ is not in Revelation 5:13. The unsaved are not in Heaven and they do not worship Jesus. They only give praise and honour, and request that glory and power be given to God and to Jesus. It is only the saved and the angels who worship Jesus. Why? The Holy Spirit does not indwell the unsaved. In John 4:23-24 we read that Jesus said, ‘“...true worshipers will worship the Father in the Spirit and in truth, for they are the kind of worshipers the Father seeks. God is spirit, and his worshipers must worship in the Spirit and in truth.”’ We cannot go into details but there is a difference between ‘worship’ and ‘praise and honour.’ As we shall read, the unsaved will acknowledge who Jesus is and God will be glorified. We must not confuse this with worship or a second chance to be saved. Paul wrote two similar statements in separate letters:

‘Jesus is Lord:’ Romans 10:9-10. ‘Say with your mouth, “Jesus is Lord.” Believe in your heart that God raised him from the dead. Then you will be saved. With your heart you believe and are made right with God. With your mouth you say that Jesus is Lord. And so you are saved.’

‘Jesus Christ is Lord:’ Philippians 2:8-11. Jesus ‘being found in appearance as a man he humbled himself by becoming obedient to death-- even death on a cross! Therefore God exalted him to the highest place and gave him the name that is above every name, that at the name of Jesus every knee should bow, in heaven and on earth and under the earth, and every tongue acknowledge that Jesus Christ is Lord...’

It seems that some believers embrace the ‘second chance’ theory because they cannot face up to the truth that their unsaved deceased close relatives and friends will endure God’s eternal punishment. But, to be totally frank, it seems that these same believers have no such difficulty accepting that others whom they do not personally know and who died unsaved will endure God’s eternal punishment for their sins. There is a similar problem because some believers:

- Hope that loved ones were saved in their last moments.
- Are overjoyed that loved ones said words similar to, “I accept Jesus as my Saviour” in their last moments.

Believers must avoid giving unbelievers the false idea that they can be saved on their deathbeds by:

- Having prayers said for them or some religious ceremony performed by a church functionary.
- Repeating some words from the Bible or a prayer book.

Believers ought to know that that not only does the Bible teach that repentance proceeds belief, Paul in Romans 10:9-10 sets out the only basis on which sinners can be saved.

'Say…mouth…' 'Believe…heart…' Romans 10:9-10.

These vital verses should be memorised. 'Say with your mouth, "Jesus is Lord." Believe in your heart that God raised him from the dead. Then you will be saved. With your heart you believe and are made right with God. With your mouth you say that Jesus is Lord. And so you are saved.' Consider these two expressions that have no exceptions:

- 'Then you will be saved.'
- 'And so you are saved.'

So you will be saved if you:

- 'Say with your mouth, 'Jesus is Lord.'
- 'Believe in your heart that God raised him from the dead.'

You must do both to be saved. They are not alternatives.

'Say with your mouth, 'Jesus is Lord.'

Question 1: Why is repentance not mentioned? Answer: 'Lord' means 'supreme in authority.' Jesus wants to be 'supreme in authority' over your life. He wants to indwell you by the Holy Spirit Who will teach you how to live a holy life.

Question 2: How could Jesus be 'supreme in authority' over someone who had not repented of their sin?

Question 3: Would anyone accept Jesus as 'supreme in authority' over them unless they were willing to give up their sinful life to live a new holy life that pleases God?

Question 4: Does the New Testament state in practical terms what it means for Jesus to be Lord in our lives? Answer: Yes. Paul wrote to the Corinthian believers, 'you do not belong to yourselves.' Paul's words are vital to a correct understanding of God's Salvation.

'You do not belong to yourselves.' 1 Corinthians 6:19.

These words clearly explain what it really means to have Jesus as your Lord. Paul lists the sins the believers committed before they were saved. He then states why they should now live differently. 'Some of you used to do those things. But your sins were washed away. You were made holy. You were made right with God. All of that was done in the name of the Lord Jesus Christ and by the Spirit of our God...Don't you know that your bodies are temples of the Holy Spirit? The Spirit is in you. You have received him from God. You do not belong to yourselves. Christ has paid the price for you. So use your bodies in a way that honors God.'

'Believe in your heart that God raised him from the dead'

Paul states in Romans 10:9-10 that to be saved a sinner needs to say with their mouth, "Jesus is Lord" and also believe in their heart that God raised Jesus from the dead. When we considered Philippians 2 we read, '...at the name of Jesus every knee should bow, in heaven and on earth and under the earth, and every tongue acknowledge that Jesus Christ is Lord, to the glory of God...' Philippians 2:10-11.

'At The Name of Jesus Every Knee Should Bow...'

When this event happens we read that:

- Every knee will bow to Jesus.
- Everyone's mouth will say that Jesus Christ is Lord.
- God the Father will receive the glory.

Question: Why is Philippians 2 silent about a belief that God raised Jesus from the dead? Answer:

- At that time it will be too late for belief because it will then be obvious that God raised Jesus from the dead.
- The time to believe the truth of Jesus' resurrection is now.

A Word of Caution: Many religions have written standard prayers that their adherents read or repeat from memory. For the sake of clarity, it is vital that you do not equate standard prayers with words that express true belief or words that come from the heart. No faith is required to read or repeat words from memory. That only involves the intellect. The Gospel's emphasis is not on our intellects, it is on our hearts.

Choice End When the Unsaved Die

The unsaved have a choice before they die.

They can acknowledge that Jesus is their Lord by accepting His divine authority over them, bowing the knee to Him and worshipping Him. Or they can continue to:

- Reject Jesus and live as they please.
- Replace the worship of Jesus with dead religious ritualism and good works.
- Worship their possessions, ambitions, sport or anything that replaces God in their lives.

The unsaved will have no choice when at the time we have read about the Name of Jesus is spoken. We know exactly what every single one of them will do. They will bow the knee to Jesus and say, "Jesus Christ is Lord." And God will be glorified. Today the unsaved:

- Blaspheme Jesus' Name and belittle Him.
- Ignore what Jesus has done for them.

The first category might not describe your present attitude to Jesus. But if the second category does, you will spend eternity with those who do blaspheme Jesus' Name and belittle Him. But you will not then have the choice of ignoring Jesus and what He achieved when He died on the cross:

- You will acknowledge that He is Lord.
- You will bow the knee to Him.
- You will give praise and honour to Jesus, the Lamb of God who died and came alive again.

Jesus died to be your Saviour but your rejection of Him means that He will be your Judge.

A Word of Caution: Man-made Rules

If Jesus is our Lord:

- ❖ there will be a contrast between what we were before we were saved and what we are now.
- ❖ there must be a contrast between our behaviour and that of the unsaved.

Regrettably, to ensure that this contrast between the saved and the unsaved exists, some churches have developed 'man-made' rules that are mandatory on their members. Disobedience results in excommunication.

Some of these church rules do mirror Biblical principles. The 'Life and Lip' rule, for example, requires that a believer's life matches their words. The reason is obvious. Unbelievers call those whose lives do not match what they preach "hypocrites." As all believers, and not just those who have the evangelist's gift, should spread the Gospel, the 'Life and Lip' rule said that the life without the lip was a mystery but the lip without the life was a tragedy.

Beware of those who live by 'man-made' rules and impose their rules on others. Men are not worthy of your obedience. We repeat Paul's words above. You will not find any 'man-made' rules in what he writes as he expresses so clearly why and how a believer must live and bring honour to God. '...your sins were washed away. You were made holy. You were made right with God. All of that was done in the name of the Lord Jesus Christ and by the Spirit of our God...Don't you know that your bodies are temples of the Holy Spirit? The Spirit is in you. You have received him from God. You do not belong to yourselves. Christ has paid the price for you. So use your bodies in a way that honors God.' 1 Corinthians 6:11 & 19-20.

Statistics and Headcounts: Jesus is Lord

If Salvation involved only people saying, "Jesus is Lord," we could count how many had said these three words and know exactly how many had been saved. But the expression, 'Jesus is Lord' is not a magic formula that turns people into believers. Unbelievers must:

- ❖ Repent and submit to Jesus' authority over them.
- ❖ Believe that God raised Jesus from the dead.

Salvation involves both the mouth and the heart:

- You might hear the mouth say, "Jesus is Lord."
- You cannot hear the heart:
    - Repent and submit to Jesus' authority.
    - Believe that God raised Jesus from the dead.

Concentrating only on what people say is as futile as it is imprudent. Experience teaches that contrary to the position at the time Paul was writing, in the English speaking Western world today, few, if any, are persecuted or executed for their religious beliefs. It is neither difficult nor dangerous for people to publically declare that, "Jesus is Lord."

The 'stumbling block' is, as it always was, repentance. We must, like Jesus, be frank about sin and sinning.' In John 3:19 we read that Jesus said, "'This is the verdict: Light has come into the world, but people loved darkness instead of light because their deeds were evil.'"

- It is both evident and regrettable that many believers have a view of sin and sinners that either contradicts Jesus' view, or is a 'toned down' version of it.
- Jesus' verdict of all unbelievers is clearly stated and He neither exaggerated nor listed exceptions.

Jesus said that unbelievers love the darkness as without exception they do evil things. It really is naïve to think that:

- Satan will easily release unbelievers from his grasp.
- Satan is retaining unbelievers against their wills.

Jesus said that unbelievers love the darkness. They:

- love their sin.
- love sinning.
- are loath to stop sinning.

Do not be misled because an unbeliever appears to be:

- Religious.
- Respectable.

To put it bluntly, 'religious sinners,' 'respectable sinners' and the like are as 'unsaved' as all other unbelievers. To single them out for 'special treatment' when evangelistic events are planned is the opposite of how Jesus dealt with them.

The verses from Romans 10 indicate that Salvation involves far more than a person saying, "Jesus is Lord," or "I believe," signing a 'Salvation card' or repeating a written prayer. That is why the New Testament teaches that only a person's changed life evidences the reality of their conversion.

'Headcounts' cannot measure 'evangelistic success.' It seems that the Bible warns believers against conducting all headcounts. Statistics cannot measure a believer's or a church's faithfulness to God. Some quote 'their church's evangelistic and baptismal success rates,' to prove that they belong to a 'spiritual church.' But when you ask how many of those who have been saved and baptised still attend the church, you often hear a statistic that can only be described as 'the church's failure rate.'

"I have sinned badly…" "I've been really stupid."

The Bible cautions against statistics. They can so easily replace trust. King David counted his fighting men. He had 1,300,000. He then realised he had sinned as 'The Message' explains so clearly. He was, 'overwhelmed with guilt because he had counted the people, replacing trust with statistics. And David prayed to GOD, "I have sinned badly in what I have just done. But now GOD forgive my guilt—I've been really stupid." 2 Samuel 24.10. The problem:

- ❖ If God asked David to fight an enemy who had mustered 650,000 men, David would have obeyed without question.
- ❖ If God asked David to fight an enemy who had mustered 2,600,000 men David would have hesitated to obey.

Without the statistics David would have trusted that if God asked him to do something, God would guarantee the result.

We really do need to question our own attitude to statistics. Have we allowed statistics to stifle God's work?

- ❖ Do we need to exceed a 'minimum number' of attendees before we proceed with evangelistic events or are we as pleased as the angels when just one sinner repents?

- ❖ Believers should be baptised but do we only baptise them 'when there are sufficient to make it worthwhile?'
- ❖ Statistics, targets and budgets 'are king' in today's world.

Believers need to consider how much they actually trust God and rely on His guidance when they plan and do His work. As we read David's words, "I have sinned badly." "I've been really stupid," do we share his sense of guilt? Are we as honest as he was to confess that when we rely on ourselves to do God's work we are as stupid as we are sinful?

But believers who have replaced trust with statistics and self-support are not the only ones who need to consider David's prayer. It gives all of us a clear example of how we can obtain God's forgiveness for our sins. David knew from experience that God was willing to forgive those who:

- ❖ Admit their sins. David confessed, "I have sinned..."
- ❖ Regret their sins. David was 'overwhelmed with guilt.'
- ❖ Ask for forgiveness. David said, "Forgive my guilt..."

God's Kindness and God's Anger. Romans 2:4-5.

It would be difficult to think of a greater contrast than God's kindness and His anger. Bear this in mind as you read. When Paul wrote to Rome he wrote to the believers. But in some parts of his letter he addresses unbelievers and he did not 'mince his words' when he wrote about their general attitude to God. 'Do you make fun of God's great kindness and favor? Do you make fun of God when he is patient with you? Don't you realize that God's kindness is meant to turn you away from your sins? But you are stubborn. In your heart you are not sorry for your sins. You are storing up anger against yourself. The day of God's anger is coming...' Romans 2:4-5. These verses need no comment from us. We have taken the last seven words of Romans 2:5 as our next heading because it seems appropriate to use them to introduce the last three verses we shall be considering from Revelation.

'THE DAY OF GOD'S ANGER IS COMING'

Death, Hell and the Lake of Fire: Revelation 20:14-15.

'...Death and Hell were thrown into the lake of fire. The lake of fire is the second death. Anyone whose name was not written in the Book of Life was thrown into the lake of fire.' Revelation 20:14-15.

'Only those.' Revelation 21:27.

'Only those whose names are written in the Lamb's Book of Life will enter the city.' Revelation 21:27. The Bible has only one Gospel message. Those who want to be saved must be sorry for their sins and repent. We let Paul have the last word on what repentance is and why it is rare despite the dreadful end that awaits those who remain unforgiven. 'Don't you realize that God's kindness is meant to turn you away from your sins. But you are stubborn. In your heart you are not sorry for your sins. You are storing up anger against yourself.' Romans 2:4-5.

Death

We have already considered the subject of death. It is 'the wages of sin.' But death is not the 'end' for those unsaved.

The Second Death

Revelation 20:14 above refers to this death. Only those who are not saved will be involved in it because those who are saved will be in Heaven. It will take place when Death and Hell are thrown into the Lake of Fire. 'Then Death and Hell were thrown into the lake of fire. The lake of fire is the second death.' Revelation 20:14.

THE LAMB'S BOOK OF LIFE

Names not written in the Book of Life. Revelation 20:15. 'Anyone whose name was not written in the Book of Life was thrown into the lake of fire.'

Names written in the Book of Life. Revelation 21:27. 'Only those whose names are written in the Lamb's Book of Life will enter the city.'

'Whose names are written in the Book of Life?' Irrespective of status, class, culture, nationality, sex, education and every other manmade division there will be:

- Names that are in the Book of Life.
- Names that are not in the Book of Life.

You decide whether your name is written in the Book of Life.

A Warning: Note the dramatic language used to describe how those who are not saved end up in the Lake of Fire?

❖ They do not enter the Lake of Fire willingly.

❖ They need to be 'thrown' into the Lake of Fire.

A Contrast

The saved do not need to be 'thrown' into Heaven. What a contrast being saved for time and eternity makes.

'The Book of Life belongs to the Lamb.' Revelation 13:8.

We can conclude our consideration of the Book of Life by remembering that it belongs to the Lamb of God who was sacrificed at Calvary. Jesus willingly suffered and died at Calvary for our sins so that you and I could freely have what we never deserved.

God's Salvation is available to you now but only you can accept or reject it. To assist you with your decision we leave you with the words of Paul, Peter and John:

PAUL wrote about sins: Romans 2:4. 'Don't you realize that God's kindness is meant to turn you away from your sins?'

PETER said about Jesus: Acts 4:12. '"You can't be saved by believing in anyone else. God has given us no other name under heaven that will save us."'

JOHN heard these words about Jesus when he had a vision of Heaven: Revelation 5:9. 'You are worthy because you were put to death. With your blood you bought people for God. They come from every tribe, language, people and nation.'

ACKNOWLEDGEMENTS AND NOTICES

The following Bible translations have assisted the author:

- Authorised or King James Version
- Contemporary English Version
- East-to Read Version
- God's Word
- Good News Bible
- Revised Standard Version
- The Living Bible
- The Message
- The NIV Family of Bibles

Some of these translations of the Bible and others can be downloaded free of charge from the following websites:

- www.e-sword.net
- www.BibleOcean.com

The author is grateful for the use of their material.

NOTICE

COPYRIGHT NOTICE

COPYRIGHT

Good News Broadcasting Association (GB)

Ranskill DN22 8NN United Kingdom

E-mail: info@gnba.net internet www.gnba.net

Other Books by the Author

Genesis

This book contains comments that should provoke all who read it to consider the events recorded and their own relationship to the God who created the world and yet wishes to be involved in and bless the daily lives of His creatures. In Genesis, God reveals the beginnings of His Plan of Salvation and tells us that although man sinned and continues to sin, God has always desired that man should repent of sin, be forgiven and return to Him. God has always offered man the opportunity to have "a new start" and God's offer is available today. Reading this Book will not only increase your knowledge of Genesis. It will challenge your attitude to God and to sin. It will teach you that you are special to God and that God wants you to live to please Him in a world that is hostile to Him and to those who have accepted His Son, the Lord Jesus Christ as their Saviour.

An Introduction to Paul's Letter to The Romans

Paul wrote most of the letters in the New Testament but he wrote to the Romans in a particular legal style. You must therefore expect him to introduce facts and evidence and argue the case for the truth he presented. He used legal words such as case, judge, judgment, defence, proof, evidence, sentence and witnesses.

Those who read the Bible soon realise that it is no ordinary book and that it is God's Word. Those who never read it are the ones who criticise it most. Some unwisely think that it contains myth and stories suitable only for children. The letter to the Romans was written by a lawyer. It would persuade anyone prepared to read it that no one need lower their intellect to find God's Truth. But there is more. Paul's letter was intended to deal with the fundamental doctrines of the Christian Faith. They were under attack and being undermined. Even the truths of the Gospel and Salvation were being challenged.

So, if you are a believer in the Lord Jesus Christ, you can

expect to read wonderful truths about why He and He alone is able to be your Saviour, why God is able to forgive your sin that He hates and give you the eternal blessings He has prepared for you. Those not yet believers will discover in Romans why they need God's Salvation and why only the Gospel can deal with the problem of sin.

The One and Only Church

An Introduction to the Acts of The Apostles

Who would have guessed that from the small group who followed Jesus, a worldwide Church would have emerged? Although so diverse, its members are all cleansed by the precious blood that Jesus shed when He suffered and died at Calvary for the sins of the world. They are forgiven because they have believed the Gospel, the good news from God that Christ died for our sins, was buried but came back to life.

They have their own story to tell as to how they were saved but when they were, they were built into the Christian Church. It began at Pentecost when the Holy Spirit indwelt those who were saved. Down the centuries for two thousand years, those who are saved have preached the Gospel so it would not be easy today to name places where the Gospel is unknown. As technology develops, broadcasts will reach wider areas and as people hear the Gospel, accept the Lord Jesus Christ as their Saviour and are saved, the Church will continue to grow.

This book looks at the early days of the Church. Every event is considered and any changes that took place are studied to see if there are lessons to be learnt. This book also considers if the Church that began two thousand years ago is relevant today and if it will survive.

The Word from John

John's Gospel Chapters 1-4

This book is primarily for those who want to know more about Jesus. John wrote about Jesus in a particularly special and unique way in his Gospel. In John 20:31 we read why John wrote his Gospel. 'These have been written in order that you may believe that Jesus is the Messiah, the Son of God, and that through your faith in him you may have life.' John intended us to believe that Jesus is God's Son and that faith in Jesus will give us life.

The first four chapters of John's Gospel contain divine truths that require careful reading and thoughtful consideration. To make the truths that John wrote understandable we avoid theological words. There are fundamental truths in John 1 and they set the scene for later chapters. John was attempting to teach divine truths in a way that we humans can understand so he used everyday words to show that Jesus was God's Son and that Jesus was unique and beyond comparison. Because Jesus had become so special to him, John wanted his readers to put their trust in Jesus and have the eternal life that Jesus promised to those who believed in Him. We also want that for you. We want to prove to you that Jesus is unique and that it is pointless trusting anyone else or anything else for Salvation.

Dr Derek Stringer, National Director, Good News Broadcasting Association (UK) writes, 'The Gospel of John is one of the greatest books of all time. We owe so much to the insights of John in giving us a clearer picture of Jesus Christ. It is no small accomplishment to present time-honoured truth in a fresh way. But this is what Harold Booth accomplishes with distinction. With a lucid style, Harold takes us into the opening chapters. There are no cliché bromides here, but rather rigorous Biblical truth presented with eyes wide open to contemporary life and practical application. Read it because it is worth it.

These and other Bible based books are available from:

Good News Broadcasting Association (GB)
Ranskill DN22 8NN United Kingdom
E-mail: info@gnba.net internet www.gnba.net